100
ATHLETES
WHO SHAPED SPORTS HISTORY

Timothy Jacobs

Russell Roberts

D1413463

A Bluewood Book

This edition produced and published
by Bluewood Books
A Division of The Siyeh Group, Inc.,
P.O. Box 689
San Mateo, CA 94401

ISBN 0-912517-53-0

Printed in U.S.A.
10, 9, 8, 7, 6, 5, 4, 3, 2, 1

Editor: Tony Napoli
Designer: Matt Medeiros
Illustrators: Vadim Vahrameev and
Zimou Larry Tan

Key to cover illustration:
Clockwise, starting from top left:
Phidippides, Bill Russell, Babe
Didrikson-Zaharias, Jerry Rice, Joe
DiMaggio, Sonja Henie, Rod Laver
and Muhammad Ali in the center.

About the Author:
Russell Roberts is a full-time
freelance writer. He has authored
over 15 books, including *Stolen! A
History of Base Stealing*. He has also
written and published more than 250
articles and short stories.
Roberts lives in Bordertown, New
Jersey with his wife, daughter and
Calico cat named Rusti. He graduated from Rider College with a degree
in journalism.

Timothy Jacobs is the author
and editor of numerous volumes
including *The Golf Courses of Robert
Trent Jones, Jr.*, *The Golf Courses of
Jack Nicklaus* and *Great Golf
Courses of the World*. Mr. Jacobs

currently resides in Northern
California with his wife and two children.

Photo Acknowledgements:
All photographs in this book are
furnished courtesy of the Bluewood
Books Archive with the exception of
the following: International Swimming
Hall of Fame: 52, 78, 95; Library of
Congress: 24, 38; Museum of
Yatching: 19; Naismith Memorial
Basketball Hall of Fame: 45, 47, 58,
61, 75, 87, 93; The National
Baseball Hall of Fame Library: 14,
17, 20, 26, 40, 42, 53, 56, 60;
Penguin Books USA: 102; United
States Golf Association: 15, 28, 29,
32, 34, 41, 51, 65, 107; Watkins
Glen Motor Racing Research Library:
59, 63, 66; World Figure Skating
Museum & Hall of Fame: 18, 33

TABLE OF CONTENTS

1. 2. 3.   4.

5.   7.
6.   8.
9. 10.

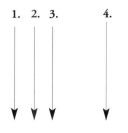
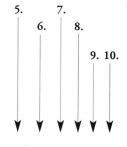

600 B.C   1875

TABLE OF CONTENTS

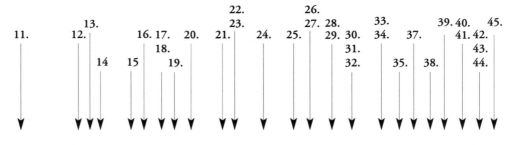

1876   1930

TABLE OF CONTENTS

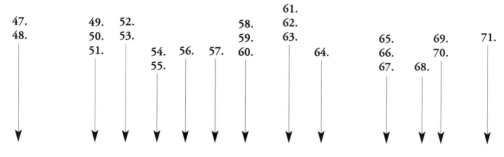

1931

1950

TABLE OF CONTENTS

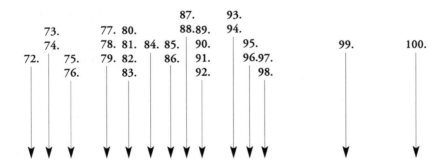

1951   **1980**

INTRODUCTION

Sports are an integral part of the human experience. Athletic competition serves as a barometer of society's progress, as well as a measure of human sacrifice, dedication, and aspiration.

This book describes the achievements of 100 extraordinary people, from all over the world, across the entire spectrum of sports. Beginning with the legendary wrestlers and runners of ancient Greece and Rome, and ending with the modern baseball and football superstars of the 21st century, these 100 biographies provide the highlights of the accomplishments of some of the most skilled and talented athletes in sports history.

In the past, organized sporting activity has tended to flourish when civilizations have matured beyond the basic survival stage—when economic and cultural development has allowed resources to be diverted into the development and training of athletes. Nations are proud of their sports heroes; they represent the vigor and vitality of their country. Whether it's an Olympian winning a gold medal, or a professional baseball player smashing home runs in a World Series game, sports fans revel in these accomplishments as a reflection of their country.

However, beyond that, we follow sports so closely because in the athletes, we see ourselves. In the image of Michael Jordan sinking a last-minute jumper, or Ted Williams lashing a game-winning hit, or Tiger Woods birdying the final hole to win a big tournament, we see ourselves. Every kid who swings a bat, throws a football, or does a somersault in the gym imagines themselves perhaps as a future Barry Bonds, Joe Montana, or Nadia Comaneci.

As for the athletes themselves, men and women such as Jim Thorpe, Jackie Robinson, Pat McCormick, Johnny Unitas, Martina Navratilova, and Lance Armstrong have proven that the desire to excel—at times despite great odds—can be a driving force within the human spirit. Many athletes sacrificed greatly, trained rigorously, and in some cases overcame great obstacles to reach the peak of athletic perfection. Perhaps that is why it is so hard for some to admit when age and injuries have taken a toll on their once-awesome skills, and acknowledge that it is time retire. It is difficult to admit that something to which you've relentlessly dedicated many years of your life is over—often at an age when most people are just reaching their prime years of life.

However, this book describes the athletic prime years of these individuals—the times when remarkable men and women accomplished feats that may have even amazed themselves while they thrilled hundreds and thousands of sports fans who witnessed them. It is about those people who, oftentimes, proved so adept or so skillful that they not only rewrote the record books, but even changed the way a game is played, or perceived. It is about, many times, perfection—and that is a rare thing to find anywhere in life.

So enjoy the stories of these 100 athletes. Admire their dedication and delight in their achievements, because in the final analysis, they are in many ways our heroes.

1. Milo of Crotona

(c. 558 B.C.) Wrestling, Weightlifting

Born in Crotona (the present-day region of Calabria in Italy) in 558 B.C., **Milo** was as large in life as most Greek heroes were in myth. His athletic career, which coincided with the era of the original Olympic Games, spanned 25 years, and brought him much notoriety. He may have been the most dominant athlete in any sport of all time. As an ancient writer put it: "Neither God nor man could stand against him!"

The image of Milo from antiquity is that of a man carrying a four-year-old heifer on his shoulders. The weight of the animal is estimated to be at least 900 pounds, and it is clear from the ancient records that Milo carried the heifer on his shoulders. This is a highly difficult lifting feat, made even harder when combined with the distance he carried the animal: the length of the Olympic stadium, which was in excess of 600 feet (approximately 630 feet today).

Milo was the wrestling champion in six Olympian, seven Pythian, nine Nemean, and 10 Isthmian Games. According to two differ-

ent accounts, he failed to win his seventh Olympics only because either wrestling was canceled when none of his competitors had the courage to show up; or, his lone competitor, an athlete named **Timastheos**, refused to come near him after her entered the wrestling arena.

Milo was considered to be the greatest of all ancient Olympian athletes. As was sometimes the practice with highly revered athletes, a huge bronze statue was created in his honor. The statue, however, had to be transported to the Altis ("high place") at Olympia, and no one could engineer a way to do it. Rather than be dishonored, Milo picked the statue up and carried it to the Altis himself.

The traditional account of Milo's death is that he found a tree that some woodcutters had partially split open with a wedge. When he tried to finish the job and tear the tree apart, the wedge fell out, and the tree closed on his hand, imprisoning him. Wolves then discovered him and devoured him.

Milo of Crotona

Phidippides
(c. 490 B.C.) Track and Field

Phidippides was an Athenian Greek. He was a trained athletic runner and messenger who set a rare example of dedication, courage, and stamina. He also unwittingly established what is now known as a **"marathon"** by running 26 miles nonstop, from the Greek city of Marathon to Athens, to bring news of the Greek victory over the Persians in the Battle of Marathon.

As a runner, Phidippides had made his mark in the ancient world just shortly before making his historic run. In 490 B.C., the Persian army had landed a large force on the plains of Marathon, just outside of Athens, and prepared to attack the Greek city. Greatly outnumbered, the Athenians decided to ask the city of Sparta for help in fighting off their enemy. The Athenian generals sent Phidippides, a professional runner, to Sparta to deliver the plea for support.

The distance between the two cities was approximately 140 miles over very mountainous and rugged terrain, but Phidippides covered it in about 36 hours. After delivering the message, Phidippides ran back to Athens with the response—Sparta agreed to help, but only when the moon was full—meaning that he ran about 280 miles in 72 hours! It should also be noted that he did this either barefoot or wearing sandals.

Knowing that they couldn't wait that long for the Spartan reinforcements, the Athenian army —including Phidippides, in full battle armor—marched out to face the Persians. They unleashed a surprise offensive that caught the Persians off-guard and defeated them. The remaining Persians set sail south, for the city of Athens, to try and capture it before the Athenian army could return there.

The Athenian army then sent Phidippides racing to Athens, to carry news of their great victory over the Persians and to warn of their approaching ships. Despite his recent efforts—running 280 miles, then fighting a battle in full armor —Phidippides ran the 26 miles to Athens in about three hours. Reaching the city, he is said to have cried, "Be happy! We have won!" He then died of exhaustion.

The stamina and courage of Phidippides are evoked whenever a runner of extraordinary marathon ability becomes well-known.

Phidippides set an inspired example for all runners to follow. That he established one of the great racing distances, and that it remains in use even today, is an "endurance record" of another kind—of almost 2,500 years!

Phidippides

3. Phayllos of Crotona
(c. 480 B.C.) Track and Field

In the ancient world, the Pentathlon was a competitive sporting event composed of the long jump, discuss throw, wrestling, 200-yard dash, and javelin throw. The most famous of all Greek athletes at this event was **Phayllos of Crotona.**

Phayllos won the Pentathlon at the Pythian Games at Delphi twice, and was also a champion runner in events apart from the Pentathlon. He performed his athletic feats within a century after **Milo of Crotona** had amazed the ancient world with his legendary athletic ability.

One of Phayllos's greatest accomplishments was making a 55-foot long jump. Even though this was in Delphic feet, which were approximately seven inches long, it still makes his jump equal to 32 feet today. What also must be taken into account is that Greek long jumpers used four-pound weights in each hand to add momentum to their jumps,

Phayllos of Crotona

although the take-off run was comparatively short, and may have offset the advantage of using weights.

Another of Phayllos's legendary feats in competition was a 95-foot discus throw. However, this is almost impossible to compare with current discus records, since the discus in Phayllos's day was made of stone, ranged in weight from 2.75 pounds to 12.5 pounds, and came in various sizes. We have to assume that ancient peoples took these variances into account when establishing championships. The Greek style of discus throwing also involved moving only one step forward, and the discus was thrown in a vertical arc.

However, we have the authority of such eminent ancient writers as **Herodotus**, **Pausanias**, **Zenobius** and **Scholion**—writing after Phayallos's time —to say that he was one of the greatest ancient athletes.

Roman Emperor Domitian
(A.D. 51-96) Archery

Of all the Roman emperors who took up the bow and arrow as a sport and practiced it seriously, Roman Emperor **Domitian** was probably one of the most important in establishing archery as a pastime.

His skill level was supposedly very high. For exhibitions, he would have a servant stand several yards away from him. The servant then held his hand out away from his body, and stretched his fingers wide. Domitian would shoot an arrow between each of the servant's fingers, without so much as grazing him.

Legend says that the emperor killed up to 100 wild animals in a single day at Alba. According to the story, he drew his bow with such skill and quickness that he could shoot two arrows in rapid succession into the head of the animal.

Domitian's proficiency with the bow and arrow inspired others to take up archery, firmly establishing it as a sport in ancient Rome. In fact, one of the emperors who succeeded him, **Commodus** (A.D. 161-192), put on archery exhibitions in the Roman arena.

This was an important milestone in the development of archery, since Romans tended

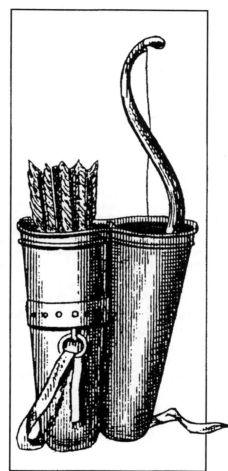

to view bows and arrows as the enemy's weapons—Greeks and Persians, for example—and not their own.

Domitian also established Greek Olympic-style games in Rome. While Greek games took place in Roman-held Greek colonies after Rome became the dominant power in the Mediterranean region, Domitian established the first regularly held Greek-style athletic contests on Roman soil.

Domitian named these games the Capitoline Games. They were immediately included in the list of Greek "Sacred Games," and were seen as second only to the Olympics themselves.

The Capitoline Games were quadrennial, and had three main contest divisions. These were music, equestrian, and gymnastics, and even included races for the maidens (women were generally forbidden from participating in the ancient Greek games). There was also singing, accompaniment, and solo-playing of instruments.

So it was, that whatever historians may think of Domitian's political rule as Roman emperor, he did make positive advancements in several realms of the sports world of his time.

5. Thomas Topham
(1710-1749) Weightlifting

Student of physical culture **David Willoughby** theorizes in his book, *The Super Athletes*, that some individuals are true prodigies, being naturally endowed to outperform the rest of us. Willoughby's conception of physical prodigies is that they are simply built differently than the rest of us—tendons are attached to bone in such a way as to give them superior muscular leverage, their glands secrete just a little more strength-giving substance than the average person—and that accounts for strength that is disproportionate to height and weight.

Thomas Topham, an 18th century British innkeeper, was a physical prodigy who demonstrated amazing strength during his short but extraordinary life.

Topham was not an overly big man; he stood 5 feet 10 inches tall and weighed 196 pounds. Yet he was the strong man upon whom all the strong men who followed have based their routines.

Topham was the son of a carpenter, and although he was trained in his father's profession, he became manager of London's Red Lion Inn at the age of 25. This was right around the time that he suffered a lifelong injury: he was restraining two draft horses in an exhibition when the ground gave way and he shattered one of his kneecaps. Remarkably enough, this serious injury was at the start of his amazing career, yet it didn't prevent him from performing some incredible feats.

Reportedly, Topham could bend an inch-thick iron poker around a man's neck like a bow tie, and then "untie" it easily, a feat he supposedly once demonstrated when a customer insulted him and Topham decided to embarrass the man.

Topham's hand strength was such that he once cracked a coconut in one hand, like a cook cracks an egg. He also could snap pipe stems in his outstretched fingers, and could crush pipe bowls by squashing them with his first and second fingers. He carried a full-grown horse over a gate, and lifted 224 pounds over his head with just his little finger. He also reportedly once lifted a 378-pound man using only one arm.

However, those feats pale before his most notable public exhibition: he performed a harness lift of 3 heavy casks weighing a total of 1,836 pounds while standing on a platform. He did this at a large celebration in honor of the British victory at the Spanish port of Cartagena on April 1, 1741.

If that was all that Topham was credited with, he would have carved out an impressive niche in the world of weightlifting. There was more, however. He supposedly carried a sleeping sentry and his sentry box several blocks to confuse the man when he woke up. He also seized hold of the rear end of horse-drawn carriage and pulled it backwards, even as the carriage's team of horses struggled to go forward. He even managed to jog for one-half mile while carrying a 336-pound barrel of nails.

Unfortunately, great physical strength does not guarantee protection against life's various trials, as Topham learned. One day he stormed out of his home following a quarrel with his wife and injured himself. He died as a result of that injury on August 10, 1749.

Sultan Selim III
(1761-1808) Archery

Sultan **Selim III** was a Turkish ruler whose archery skills were so great that he set a record in the sport that lasted almost two centuries.

Traditionally, archery has sometimes been the sport of emperors and kings; the Roman Emperor **Domitian** (see no. 4), was a noted archer in the 1st Century A.D. The Turkish Court during the Ottoman Empire, in particular, took this tradition very seriously. The Turkish bow was also more than just a weapon; it was associated with sacred and symbolic functions. The sons of Ottoman sultans learned a skill associated with the bow and arrow that they often continued to practice when they became rulers.

Selim III's skill was as a bow maker. Thus he was a natural candidate to settle a simmering dispute between the English and Turks about archery in 1798.

Two years earlier, a Turkish ambassador visiting England had boasted loudly that Turkish bows were better than English bows. The English, who trace their "archery ancestry" back to ancient times, proposed that the ambassador prove

his boast.

The Turkish ambassador agreed; he selected an old bow from the era of the Seljuk Turks (1000-1300) and shot an arrow from it. The arrow traveled 482 yards—which at the time would have been a long distance record with a modern bow.

This incident was still on everyone's mind in 1798 when Sultan Selim III decided to set the matter straight once and for all in front of the British ambassador, Sir **Robert Ainslie**.

The sultan unsheathed an arrow and placed it on his bow—quite probably one he had made himself, given his background. He then most likely set himself in the "freestyle" method—in which the archer lies on his back, braces his feet against the bow, and pulls the string back with both hands—and let the arrow fly.

The arrow soared an incredible 972 yards and 2.75 inches. Ainslie himself confirmed the distance, which was a world record. It remained a world record for almost two hundred years.

Unfortunately for the sultan, his record made out better than he did. He was deposed in 1807, and executed in 1808.

Sultan Selim III

1. Cy Young
(1867-1955) Baseball

Denton True "Cyclone" Young was one of the greatest pitchers in baseball history. In his long career (1890-1911) he won an incredible 511 games—a total that remains the most in major league history and a record that is likely never to be broken.

Young was born in Gilmore, Ohio, in 1867. He supposedly received his unique nickname one day when he was warming up by throwing the ball against a cyclone fence, and severely damaged the fence. Eventually Cyclone was shortened to Cy, and it stuck.

Despite his exceptional fast-ball, most base-ball scouts originally dismissed Young as a real pitching prospect. However, legendary hitter and future Hall of Famer **Cap Anson** thought differently. When Young beat Anson's team on August 6, 1890 for his first major league victory, Anson tried to buy Young's contract from the Cleveland Spiders of the National League for $1,000.

Fortunately for Cleveland, they rejected Anson's offer, because Young was on the verge of a remarkable career. After winning 9 games in 1890, Young blossomed the next season, reeling off 27 victories. He then notched 36 wins in 1892, with an outstanding 1.93 earned run average. He later went on to compile victory totals of 34, 35, and 28 during the decade of the 1890s.

In 1901, the new American League was formed as competition for the established National League. One way the new league challenged the older one was to sign some of its star players. Young gave the upstart league instant credibility when he jumped to the Boston Pilgrims (the present-day Red Sox).

Young was thought to be near the end of his career when he joined Boston, but the man known for his endurance on the mound wasn't nearly through yet. In his first four seasons with Boston, he won 33, 32, 28 and 26 games. In 1903, he helped pitch Boston to an upset victory against the Pittsburgh Pirates in major league baseball's first World Series. In 1904, Young accomplished the most difficult feat for a pitcher by hurling a perfect game against the Philadelphia Athletics.

Cy Young

Although it seemed like Young could go on forever, even he eventually had to defer to Father Time. In 1911, after a 7-9 season, the 44-year-old Young retired to his farm near Peoli, Ohio. Remarkably, despite pitching more than 7,000 innings in his career, Young boasted that he had never had a sore arm or required so much as a rubdown.

Young was voted into the baseball Hall of Fame in 1937. Major league baseball's annual award for the best pitcher in each league is named after him.

8. Harry Vardon
(1870-1937) Golf

Harry Vardon is one of the most revered figures in golf history. In addition to winning six British Open championships from 1896 to 1914, he was the runner-up in that tournament four times.

Unlike many other great golfers, Vardon did not grow up in a golfing environment. He worked as a gardener for a man who enjoyed golf and who sometimes let him caddie. Vardon's employer would also let him use his equipment to play a few strokes. Curious as to his level of skill, Vardon entered a few tournaments. When he won one and finished second in the other, he turned professional.

In 1896, at Muirfield in East Lothian, Scotland, Vardon defeated **J.H. Taylor** 157 to 161 in 36 holes to win his first British Open. He was the first Englishman to win the tournament.

In 1900, Vardon visited the United States. That year, at the U.S. Open at the Chicago Golf Club in Wheaton, Illinois, he beat Taylor again to win that tournament. Vardon went on to tour the country, won all but one of 88 exhibitions he played, and helped popularize the growth of golf in America.

In 1913, Vardon made a second visit to the United States and entered that year's U.S. Open, which was held at the Country Club in Brookline, Massachusetts. In one of golf's greatest matches, Vardon was tied at the end of regulation play with Englishman **Ted Ray** and an up and coming 20-year-old American named **Francis Ouimet**. The next day, Vardon finished runner-up to Ouimet, who won the 18-round playoff.

Vardon was golf's first international celebrity and is credited with devising the first modern golf swing. He was also said to be a crusty man who didn't mince words. A story has it that he was playing a round of golf with 18-year-old **Bobby Jones** (see no. 21) in Toledo, Ohio. Though later a man of grace and quiet self-control, Jones had a perfectionist's bad temper when he was young.

Vardon and Jones were playing fairly even when the brash young Jones knocked his ball into a bunker. In disgust Jones turned to Vardon and said, "Did you ever see a worse shot?" Vardon then spoke for the first and last time that day: "No." From that day forward Jones learned to control his emotions.

In 1920, at the age of 50 and following two bouts with tuberculosis, Vardon tied for second place in the USGA Open. In addition to his outstanding play over the years, Vardon also did course alterations, such as at the great Irish Royal County Down course in Newcastle.

Harry Vardon

15

9. Ray Ewry
(1873-1937) Track and Field

Ray Ewry was truly an amazing athlete. He overcame a childhood disease that left him confined to a wheelchair to become a champion athlete and winner of 10 Olympic gold medals.

Ewry was born in 1873, in Lafayette, Indiana. He contracted polio when he was young, and he was told by his doctor that he would never be able to walk or move about on his own. Despite this dire prediction, Ewry set up his own exercise regimen. He gradually built up the strength in his legs, and became so mobile and athletic that he played football and went on to compete in track and field at Purdue University.

Ray Ewry

After he graduated from Purdue, Ewry moved to New York City, where he joined the New York Athletic Club (NYAC) and competed in track and field.

Ewry was one of several NYAC athletes to compete in the 1900 Olympics in Paris, France. On July 16, 1900, he won gold medals in three events: the standing high jump, standing long jump, and standing triple jump. Four years later, he won gold medals in the same three events at the Olympics held in the United States, in St. Louis, Missouri.

The standing triple jump was eliminated from the Olympics after the 1904 Games, but Ewry kept competing. He won gold medals in the standing high jump and standing long jump in 1906. Because those victories occurred outside the regular four-year Olympic Games cycle, they were not regarded as part of the official record.

However, it mattered little to Ewry. He again won gold in the standing high jump and standing long jump in the 1908 Olympics. He tried again for the Olympics in 1912, but he did not make the team.

The standing jumps were regular AAU events in Ewry's time. Often, standing jump athletes held weights in their hands to add momentum. The following are some of Ewry's best performances without weights: a standing high jump of 5 feet, in Paris in 1906; a mark of 34 feet, 8 and 1-2 inches in Paris in 1906 in the standing hop, step and jump; and, in New York City that same year, he jumped 11 feet, 6 inches in the standing broad jump.

After failing to make the Olympic team in 1912, Ewry retired from athletics and became an engineer. He died in 1937. In 1974, he was inducted into the National Track and Field Hall of Fame, and in 1983 was made a member of the U.S. Olympic Hall of Fame.

10. Honus Wagner
(1874-1955) Baseball

Honus Wagner, nicknamed the **"Flying Dutchman"** because of his speed on the bases, was one of the greatest all-around players in baseball history.

Born John Peter Wagner in 1874, in Carnegie, Pennsylvania, his professional baseball experience began with a team in Steubenville, Ohio; within two years his exceptional play had attracted the attention of **Barney Dreyfus**, owner of the Louisville Colonels of major league baseball's National League. Dreyfus signed Wagner to play for Louisville in 1897. In 61 games that year, he hit .338, and followed that the next two seasons with averages of .299 and .336.

However, the Colonels folded after the 1899 season and Dreyfus took Wagner to Pittsburgh to play with the Pirates, which he also owned. Wagner never played for another team, remaining with them for the rest of his 21-year career.

Wagner was an immediate success with Pittsburgh, hitting .381 in 1900, to lead the National League in batting for the first of eight times. Over the next 13 seasons, Wagner never failed to hit better than .300, and three times he batted better than .350. During those years he also led the league in doubles eight times, slugging average six times, and RBI four times.

Although he was extremely bowlegged, Wagner possessed great speed and used it as an offensive weapon. He stole 35 bases or more ten straight years, and led the league five times. He finished his career with 722 steals, good for tenth on the all-time list.

While he is now considered one of the greatest shortstops ever to play the game, it took Wagner several seasons to get situated at that position. He initially played every position except catcher before settling in at shortstop.

Wagner helped the Pirates win two pennants—in 1903 and 1909. Although he hit only .222 in the 1903 World Series as the Pirates fell to the Boston Red Sox, he rebounded to post a .333 average in 1909 as the Pirates beat **Ty Cobb** and the Detroit Tigers.

Known for his humility, Wagner never once argued for more money at contract time. In fact, he supposedly turned down one pay raise because he felt it was too much.

After hitting just .265 in 74 games in 1917, Wagner hung up his spikes. He retired with a .327 lifetime batting average and 3,418 hits.

Honus Wagner

Wagner returned to the Pirates as a coach in 1933, remaining with the club until 1951. He was one of the first five members inducted into baseball's Hall of Fame in 1936.

17

11. Ulrich Salchow
(1877-1949) Figure Skating

A superb figure skater who won 10 men's world championships, **Ulrich Salchow** also invented a skating maneuver that is still prominently used by skaters today: the **Salchow Jump**.

He was born Karl Emil Julius Ulrich Salchow in 1877, in Stockholm, Sweden. He won the first of his world championships in 1901, and then reeled off a string of four more championships from 1902-1905. Salchow's streak was broken in 1906, but he came back to win five more consecutive championships, from 1907-1911. He was also the first athlete to win an Olympic gold medal for skating in 1908.

Ulrich Salchow

The skating maneuver Salchow invented is one of the most difficult in the sport. In the Salchow Jump, the skater takes off from the rear inside edge of one skate, completes one, two or three revolutions, and lands on the rear outside edge of the skate. The jump is varied by the number of revolutions the skater makes; for example, a "triple Salchow" would involve three revolutions.

Salchow was also involved in other sports, and from 1919 to 1932, he served on the Swedish Amateur Boxing Committee. He also served as president of the International Skating Union from 1935-37. He died in Stockholm on April 19, 1949.

12. Harold Vanderbilt
(1884-1970) Yachting

He was the great-grandson of American railway and shipping baron **Cornelius Vanderbilt**, but more significantly for the sports world, **Harold S. Vanderbilt** was a superb yachtsman.

Harold Vanderbilt was born in 1884 into a world of nearly unprecedented luxury because of his family's wealth. As a young man, he decided to focus his energies on yacht racing instead of the family business, which was running the New York Central Railroad. Yacht racing in the 19th and early 20th centuries featured professional pilots, but Vanderbilt changed that. He was an amateur who won the America's Cup—the World Series of yacht racing—three times for the New York Yacht Club. Since Vanderbilt's time, yacht racing has witnessed the continued dominance of amateur pilots.

It was fitting that this new kind of pilot would command a new type of racing yacht, built in tune with a new classification. The boats that Vanderbilt piloted to victory were the new "J" boats, named for their sequence in the classifications. The "J" boats had 75-87 foot waterlines and featured single, massive triangular mainsails with overlapping jibs, and, later on, a parachute spinnaker as well.

Vanderbilt proposed further innovations on the 80-foot-long *Enterprise*, the J-boat he would pilot to win his first America's Cup in 1930. These innovations included a unique "Park Avenue" boom, with runners and slides that would allow aerodynamic shaping of the mainsail, and a 162-foot mainmast made of two hollow tubes of lightweight duralumin, which was half the weight of a conventional mast. Other innovations included a unique double centerboard to help both in sailing into the wind and in running before the wind, and more than two dozen winches to handle the ship's lines.

The *Enterprise* beat Irish tea merchant Sir **Thomas Lipton's** boat *Shamrock V* in the 1930 America's Cup races; the cup went to the winner of the best four out of seven. However, when international opinion rose up against *Enterprise*, Vanderbilt built a new boat—*Rainbow*. This yacht beat Englishman **Thomas Sopwith's** boat *Endeavour* four races to two.

The greatest J-boat was Vanderbilt's *Ranger*, which due to the Great Depression, was built at cost by a shipyard and fitted with rigging from Vanderbilt's two previous J-boats. This yacht beat Sopwith's *Endeavour II* four straight races in 1937.

The deepening Depression, the advent of World War II, and the after-tax structure spelled the end for the extravagant J-boats. Yachting, however, was not Harold Vanderbilt's only passion; he is also credited with inventing the game of **Contract Bridge**.

Harold Vanderbilt

13. Ty Cobb
(1886-1961) Baseball

Ty Cobb

Tyrus Raymond Cobb was a demon on the base paths, a warrior at the plate, and a fierce competitor in anything he attempted. Quite simply, he was one of the greatest baseball players of all time.

Cobb was born in Narrows, Georgia; after he achieved success as a major leaguer, legendary sportswriter **Grantland Rice** dubbed him the **Georgia Peach**. Cobb's father wanted him to be a doctor or lawyer, but Cobb wanted to play baseball instead. Playing in the minors, he was leading the league in hitting when his father was killed—shot to death by Cobb's mother, who believed him to be an intruder. Some believe it was this incident that stoked the competitive fires in Cobb to a near-volcanic level.

Cobb was bought by major league baseball's Detroit Tigers of the American League in the middle of the 1905 season. Although he hit only .240 that year, he soon became one of the most feared batters in the league. Throughout his 23-year career he hit over .400 three times, didn't hit lower than .368 from 1909-1919, and won 12 batting titles, including 9 in a row.

On the bases Cobb was as good as he was at the plate. In 1915, he stole 96 bases, a record that lasted for nearly 50 years. Overall he stole 892 bases in his career, another record that wasn't broken for five decades. He also stole home 50 times, and this mark will likely remain unbroken.

However, if speed was a big part of Cobb's game, so was how he used that speed. He was an intimidating force on the base paths, launching himself like a guided missile into the bag. If the defender happened to get into the way, so much the better, Cobb felt. It was widely suspected that he sharpened his spikes in order to scare opponents—and inflict an injury.

This combative personality carried over to his abysmal relationships with teammates and other players. Cobb's fiery, argumentative personality and will to win at any cost prevented him from becoming "one of the boys" and fitting in with the other players. The result was that he was shunned by virtually everyone in the game.

Cobb retired after the 1928 season. In his career, he amassed 4,191 hits, a record that lasted for more than half a century; his lifetime batting average of .367 is the highest in the history of the game.

In 1936, Cobb became one of the first five players elected to the baseball Hall of Fame. Although shrewd investments made him rich, he led a reclusive life after he retired, mainly because of his difficult personality. He died in Atlanta, Georgia on July 17, 1961.

14. Jim Thorpe
(1888-1953) Track and Field, Football

At the 1912 Olympic Games, the King of Sweden said to **Jim Thorpe** what everyone else in the world was thinking: "Sir, you are the greatest athlete in the world."

Today, more than a half-century after his death, many people consider James Francis Thorpe the best all-around athlete of all time.

Thorpe was born near present-day Prague, Oklahoma, but which at the time was Indian Territory. His ancestry was part **Sac and Fox Indian**, as well as part Irish and part Welsh. His original Native American name was **Wa-tho-huck** (Bright Path).

In 1907, Thorpe attended the Carlisle Indian School in Pennsylvania. He made a name for himself in football and track, but left the school in 1909 and went to North Carolina. There he played semipro baseball.

In 1911, he returned to Carlisle. His play on the varsity football team was the major reason that Carlisle beat some of the best college teams of the era. He made the All-American team in 1911 and 1912.

Thorpe excelled in other sports as well during this period. He could high-jump 6 feet 5 inches, pole vault 11 feet, run the 100-yard dash in 10 seconds flat and the 220-yard dash in 21.8 seconds. He also threw the discus 136 feet, the javelin 163 feet, and the hammer 140 feet, and ran the mile in 4 minutes, 35 seconds.

In 1912, Thorpe went to the Olympic Games in Stockholm, Sweden as a member of the U.S. team. He won gold medals in both the pentathlon and the decathlon. However, in 1913 the Amateur Athletic Union learned of his time playing semipro baseball in North Carolina, and they stripped him of his medals.

Jim Thorpe

Thorpe joined major league baseball's New York Giants in 1913. A weak hitter, he never excelled at the game, and retired in 1919. However, Thorpe's real love was football and at that he was a star. In 1915, he had organized the Canton Bulldogs professional football team and he played for them for a then-lordly $500 per game. He was an excellent runner, a fine passer, and a terrific kicker.

In 1920, the American Professional Football Association was established, with Thorpe as the first president; it became the National Football League in 1922. Thorpe played with the Bulldogs until he retired in 1929. He subsequently acted in movies, lectured on Native American culture, and served in the U.S. Merchant Marine.

In 1950, Thorpe was selected as the greatest all-around athlete and football player of the first half of the 20th century by nearly 400 American broadcasters and sportswriters. In 1982, the International Olympic Committee posthumously restored his Olympic medals.

Tazio Nuvolari's skill behind the wheel was legendary. Known as *Il Montavani Volante*—the **Flying Mantuan**—he won 30 of the most important races held in Europe between 1921 and 1939.

Nuvolari was born in 1892, in Casteldrio, near Mantua, Italy and got his start racing motorcycles at age 28. At the Monza Grand Prix for motorcycles he broke both his legs during practice. Despite being told that it would be a month before he could walk again, Nuvolari raced the next day by tying himself to the bike. He won the race.

In 1924, at the age of 32, Nuvolari began racing automobiles. In the 1930 *Mille Miglia* (Thousand Miles) he caught the unsuspecting leader while driving at night without his headlights. Three kilometers from the finish line Nuvolari suddenly pulled alongside his rival, smiled at him, flicked on his headlights, and roared to victory.

Perhaps Nuvolari's greatest victory came in the 1935 Grand Prix of Germany. Driving an aging red Alfa-Romeo, he was up against the fastest race cars in the world, the 180 mph Auto-Union cars, and the 175 mph Mercedes Benzes, driven by some of the best drivers in Europe. His Alfa was 20 mph slower.

It was a mountainous course with 175 curves, measuring 14 miles per lap. By the tenth lap, Nuvolari had risen from sixth to first place. Then his crew bungled a refueling stop, dropping him back to sixth place. By the 13th lap Nuvolari had regained second, and was pushing the first place car so hard that it ran its tires ragged and had a blowout halfway through the last lap. Nuvolari roared on by to win by 32 seconds.

Throughout his career Nuvolari drove in 172 races; he won 64 of them, placed second 16 times and third 9 times against the toughest competition of his era. Nuvolari had a tremendous desire to win—even at the cost of jeopardizing his health. In 1947, he drove for Ferrari and won twice, despite being hypersensitive to racing fuel because of tuberculosis. His lungs hemorrhaged.

Despite his illness, Nuvolari almost won the *Mille Miglia* a third time; water in his magneto slowed his car within sight of the finish line, allowing the second place driver to pass him. In 1948, he was 30 minutes ahead of the competition in the *Mille* when his Ferrari broke down. Two years later he won at Monte Pellegrino, but had to be lifted out of his car, spitting blood.

On August 11, 1953, nine months after suffering a stroke, Nuvolari died. He was buried in his uniform—a yellow jersey and blue trousers.

Tazio Nuvolari

16. Bill Tilden
(1893-1953) Tennis

Bill Tilden dominated men's tennis during much of the 1920s as no player has before or since. No wonder he was named as the greatest player of all time by an international panel of tennis writers in 1969.

Born in Pennsylvania in 1893, William Tatem Tilden Jr. entered his first tournament at the age of eight. Tennis though, was not his first love at that time. He preferred to read and listen to music.

When Tilden was 20, however, he was practicing his game on a grass court one day when he was spotted by U.S. Women's Singles champion **Mary K. Browne**. Impressed, Browne asked him to team with her for the National Mixed Doubles Championship. They won, and Tilden had found his life's calling.

Tilden played steadily throughout the next few years, including a classic series of confrontations with arch-rival **William Johnston** of California. Johnston's powerful forehand shots were pitted against Tilden's rocket-like, flat service.

After losing to Johnston in 1919, Tilden took the winter off to work on his backhand, the weakest part of his game. When he returned in 1920, Tilden became the most dominating player the sport had ever known.

In 1920, despite a knee tendon injury, Tilden became the first American to win England's Wimbledon Championship. That year, he also defeated Johnston in five sets to win the U.S. Championship at Forest Hills, New York, in one of the greatest matches in history. The score was 6-1, 1-6, 7-5, 5-7, 6-3.

Tilden then reeled off a streak of unparalleled dominance in tennis. From 1920-1926, he was virtually unbeatable in the United States; he won the U.S. Championship six straight times, won Wimbledon both times he participated, and led the United States to seven consecutive Davis Cup titles, where he

Bill Tilden

competed against some of the best players in the world.

Tilden's amateur record from 1912-1930 was an incredible 138-28. His match record was a mind-boggling 907-62. He was in the World Top Ten from 1919 through 1930, ranked number one a record six times (1920-1925), and in the U.S. Top Ten for 12 straight years, beginning in 1918.

In 1931, Tilden embarked upon a professional playing career. His name and reputation revived the languishing sport of professional tennis. For years he traveled across the country day and night, sometimes going on the court only a few hours after arriving in town.

Tilden also acted and wrote screenplays and novels. Yet tennis remained his first love. His bags were packed for a trip to play in a tournament in Cleveland when he was found dead in his room of a heart attack on June 5, 1953.

Babe Ruth
(1895-1948) Baseball

Babe Ruth

Despite the fact that many of his records have been broken, the legend of **Babe Ruth** only grows as the years go on. No baseball player ever has, or ever will be, his equal.

Even many people who aren't baseball fans are familiar with his story. He was born George Herman Ruth in Baltimore in 1895, and was an incorrigible youngster. Eventually he was sent to a home for wayward youths where he learned to play baseball—very well. He was signed by the minor league Baltimore Orioles, where he became known as the team's "Babe."

The Orioles wound up selling Ruth to the Boston Red Sox, where he became a sensational pitcher. He won 23 games in 1916 and 24 games in 1917. He helped the Red Sox win the World Series in 1916 and again in 1918. When he didn't pitch, he played the outfield, and as a hitter he showed flashes of home run power.

Then Boston owner, **Harry Frazee**, need-ing money, sold Ruth to the New York Yankees after the 1919 season. The Yankees wanted Ruth for his big bat, not his pitching. They put him in the outfield, stood back, and watched the homers fly out of the park at a record-setting rate.

In his first year with the Yankees, Ruth hit 54 homers—more than any other American League team. This was in the so-called "dead ball" era, when most games were low scoring affairs. Most people thought 54 homers was a record that would stand forever.

Ruth himself proved how wrong they were when he blasted 59 homers the next year. In 1927, he hit 60 home runs, a record that would stand until 1961. Overall in his career, the **Sultan of Swat** belted 714 home runs—another mark that was not broken until years later, in 1974.

However, it wasn't only his home runs that made Ruth a larger-than-life figure. He played hard and he lived hard, eating, drinking, and enjoying many a late night on the town. He also loved children, and would frequently visit orphans and sick kids in the hospital. A large, gregarious, friendly man, he was always ready with a quip. In 1928, after signing a contract that paid him more money than the president, Ruth explained, "I had a better year than he did."

Enormously popular with fans, Ruth single-handedly rescued baseball after the disgrace of the Black Sox betting scandal of 1919. Because of him, baseball enjoyed a Golden Age during the 1920s. During his career, Ruth's Yankees won seven pennants and four world championships.

Ruth died of throat cancer in 1948.

18. Jack Dempsey
(1895-1983) Boxing

He was a gentle man outside the boxing ring. However, when he donned his gloves, he became the **Manassa Mauler**, doing a rhythmic, shuffling dance and humming an almost inaudible tune, whose beat was the cadence of his punches.

He was born **William Harrison Dempsey** in the mining town of Manassa, Colorado in 1895. Although he worked full shifts in the mines as a teenager, his real goal was to be a prizefighter. Setting out on his own, he fought in the back room of saloons. In 1917, he linked up with manager **Jack "Doc" Kearns**, who arranged fights with top-ranked heavyweights for Dempsey.

Dempsey won 21 fights in 1918—17 by knockout. The following year, the 187-pound Dempsey fought 245-pound **Jess Willard** for the championship. He knocked Willard down seven times in the first round. By the third round, Willard conceded defeat. Later, Dempsey's manager, who was bitter after legal battles with the fighter, claimed that he had loaded Dempsey's gloves with plaster of Paris. However, sportswriters who later tested that claim found that the plaster would, if anything, have softened Dempsey's blows.

In 1921, the crafty Kearns used a charge that Dempsey had been a World War I draft dodger to stage the first million dollar prizefight in history, between Dempsey and war hero **Georges Carpentier**. Carpentier lost in four rounds, and the draft-dodging charge was later disproved in court.

In 1923, one of the most ferocious heavyweight bouts of the 20th century took place, between Dempsey and **Luis Firpo**, "the Bull of the Pampas." In the first round alone, Firpo dropped Dempsey seconds into the fight, Dempsey knocked Firpo down six times, and then Firpo knocked Dempsey completely out of the ring. In the second round, the champ knocked Firpo out.

In 1926, after three years of inactivity, Dempsey lost his title in a decision to **Gene Tunney**, who out-boxed him. In the return match the following year, Dempsey knocked Tunney down for what has become known as "the long count." Tunney was actually down for 14 seconds, but because Dempsey failed to go to a neutral corner, the referee delayed the count. This gave Tunney time to recover, and he later won the bout.

After the second fight with Tunney, Dempsey retired. He won 60 pro bouts during his career, 49 by knockout, while losing only 7. In 1950, he was voted the best Boxer of the Half-Century by an Associated Press poll.

Dempsey went on to represent the boxing world as a public figure, and to referee some fights. He also ran a well-known and popular restaurant in New York City for many years.

Jack Dempsey

Rogers Hornsby
(1896-1963) Baseball

He is often considered the greatest right-handed hitter in baseball history, but his irascible personality caused many to shun him.

Rogers Hornsby was born in Winters, Texas; his unusual first name came from his mother, whose maiden name was Rogers. She was a big baseball fan and encouraged him to play even when he didn't initially show much promise.

Hornsby eventually showed that his mother's faith was not misplaced. Purchased by the National League's St. Louis Cardinals, he led the league in slugging percentage in 1917 and hit .327—second in the league.

In 1920, Hornsby hit .370, leading the league and beginning a string of six consecutive batting titles. The following year he hit .397 with 126 runs batted in, and in 1922 he hit for a .401 average. In 1924, he had his highest average ever, hitting an astonishing .424, a 20th century National League record. Hornsby averaged over .400 from 1920-1925, and hit below .361 just once—in 1926—during the entire decade of the 1920s.

Hornsby's dislike of pitchers was legendary. "You might not have liked what was on his mind," said an opposing pitcher, "but you always knew damned well what it was."

Hornsby kept his batting eye clear and sharp by not going to the movies or reading newspapers, and his knowledge of the strike zone was so precise that even umpires deferred to it. Once a pitcher threw three close pitchers to Hornsby that were called balls. When the pitcher complained that some of the pitches were strikes, the ump responded, "Young man, when you throw a strike Mr. Hornsby will let you know."

In addition to hitting for high averages, Hornsby also displayed remarkable power for a second baseman. He slammed 42 home runs for St. Louis in 1922, and hit 301 homers during his career. In 1931, he became the first major league player to connect for a pinch-hit, grand slam home run.

As good a player as he was, Hornsby was difficult and unpleasant as a person. Driven by his intense desire to excel, he was not an easy person to know and had few friends in baseball. He even postponed his own mother's funeral so it wouldn't interfere with his participation in the 1926 World Series.

Because of his personality, Hornsby played for numerous teams throughout his career, including the Cardinals, Braves, Cubs, Giants, and Browns. He also managed several teams, including the 1926 Cardinals, who won the world championship that year. Hornsby eventually wore out his welcome—with players, managers, and owners—just about everywhere he went.

Rogers Hornsby

Paavo Nurmi, nicknamed the **"Flying Finn,"** was an exceptional long-distance runner. He set 23 world records from 1921-1931, in events ranging from the 1,500 meter to the 20,000 meter.

Nurmi was born in Abo, Finland in 1897, to a poor family. Although he had to work at an early age, he still found time to run and to display exceptional promise. In World War I, Nurmi became a soldier, yet he continued to train as a runner. He was a common sight in the early morning, running for several miles along the icy roads and returning in time for reveille.

Once the war ended, Nurmi began systematic note-taking, comparing his time with the times of other runners, and calculating exactly at which points in a race to simply stride, and when to run his fastest. He often carried a stopwatch in practice and in the more important races, which he would use to time his progress. (He threw the watch away as he began the final lap.)

Before Nurmi began using these methods, most runners would usually jog until the last two laps, and then pour all they had into the finish. However, Nurmi's use of a stopwatch enabled him to pace himself and run at a consistent speed. His methods had a great influence on the development of the sport of competitive running.

At the 1920 Olympics, Nurmi won gold medals in the 10,000-meter race and the 10,000-meter cross-country race. In addition, he led the Finnish squad to victory in the team category of that latter event.

In June 1921, Nurmi set world records for the 10,000-meter (30:40.2) and the 6-mile run (28:41.2). Over the next two years, he added three more records: the 5,000-meter (14:35.2), 1,500-meter (3:52.6), and the mile (4:10.4).

At the 1924 Olympic Games, Finnish offi-

Paavo Nurmi

cials actually prevented Nurmi from competing in the 10,000-meter race to allow other Finnish runners a chance. Nevertheless Nurmi won 5 gold medals at those Olympics, including the 1,500- and 5,000-meter races, which he won despite the fact that they were run only 55 minutes apart!

Nurmi won the gold medal in the 10,000-meter race in the 1928 Olympics, and went on to set records in distance running up until July, 1931, when he ran two miles in a record 8:59.5. He was not allowed to compete in the 1932 Olympics because it was ruled that he had lost his amateur status when he had accepted expense money for training. His last victory in a race came in 1933 at the Finnish National Championship.

21. Bobby Jones
(1902-1971) Golf

Bobby Jones

Considered by many to be the greatest golfer in history, **Bobby Jones** is the only player to win the sport's fabled grand slam. (At the time, the grand slam consisted of winning the U.S. Open, the British Open, the U.S. Amateur and the British Amateur championships in the same year.) When he retired from the game, he founded one of golf's most prestigious tournaments.

He was born Robert Tyre Jones, Jr., in 1902 in Atlanta, Georgia. He took up golf only when his parents moved near the Atlanta Country Club. Jones mastered the game quickly, however; when he was 9 he was the AAC'S junior champion, and at age 14 he entered his first U.S. Amateur tournament.

As a young man Jones had a fiery temper that hurt his game, but help from his colleagues enabled him to control it. Thereafter he was the epitome of a perfect gentleman out on the links.

Jones won the first of four U.S. Open titles in 1923, but he still felt that he was struggling as a golfer. That was when he decided that he was worrying too much about the competition. Thereafter he became determined to only worry about achieving par, and launched himself on a string of remarkable victories.

Jones won the U.S. Open in 1926, 1929 and 1930, was U.S. Amateur champion five times (1924, 1925, 1927, 1928, and 1930), and won the British Open in 1926, 1927, and 1930. In 1926, he became the first player to notch victories in both the U.S. and British Opens in the same year. He was also the only player in history ever to win both national amateur and open tournaments in both countries when he accomplished the feat in 1930.

Among Jones's many feats was a round of golf that has been described as perfect as humanly possible. During the 1926 British Open, he shot a 66 (par was 72), divided evenly between going out and coming back. He tallied 6 fours and 3 threes on each nine, or 33 putts and 33 other strokes.

Jones did all of this as an amateur, often playing against the best professionals in the world. He was especially beloved by the golf-loving Scots.

After winning the grand slam in 1930, Jones retired from active competition. In 1934, he helped design the Augusta National Golf Course in Augusta, Georgia and established the Masters Tournament to be hosted there.

Jones was named to the Professional Golfers Association Hall of Fame in 1940. After his death in 1971, he was elected to the World Golf Hall of Fame.

22. Glenna Collett-Vare
(1903-1989) Golf

A winner of a record six U.S. Women's amateur titles, **Glenna Collett-Vare** did much to put women's golf on an equal "par" with the men's game.

Born in 1903 in Connecticut, Glenna Collett grew up in Providence, Rhode Island as an accomplished athlete; she was proficient at swimming and diving, as well as baseball and tennis. At age 14, her father introduced her to golf at the Metacomet Golf Club in Providence.

Although she became quite good at the game, Collett played golf strictly for the enjoyment and the challenge. It was an attitude that she would keep toward the game her entire life, despite her great success at the sport.

At the age of 19, she won the first of her six U.S. Women's Amateur Championships. In 1923 and 1924 she won the Canadian Ladies' Championship. Even after the Ladies' Professional Golf Association (LPGA) was formed, she retained her amateur standing because she didn't want the tedium of playing every week. She recorded 49 amateur championships throughout her career, and had 19 consecutive victories between 1928-1931.

Collett-Vare—she married **Edwin Vare** in her young adulthood—was often compared to **Bobby Jones** (see no. 21), who also only competed as an amateur. Jones once said of her: "It is especially a treat to watch Glenna Collett. Her accuracy with the spoon and brassie is to me the most important part of her well-rounded game."

Among Collett-Vare's most famous accomplishments was winning her sixth National Amateur title in 1935, after a two-year lay-off to have children. She was playing against such younger stars as **Marian McDougal, Betty Jameson**, and **Patty Berg** (see no. 34). This was her 14th national tournament.

Collett-Vare continued to win tournaments at an age when most golfers were retired; she notched a victory in the Rhode Island State Championship at the age of 56. Even when she was 80, she maintained a 15 handicap and competed in the Point Judith Invitational.

Glenna Collett-Vare blazed a path that helped other women golfers succeed in what was once considered a male-dominated sport.

Glenna Collett-Vare

A legendary running back in college, **Harold Edward "Red" Grange**, also did more than almost any other player to put the National Football League, and professional football, on the map for the sporting public.

Born in Forksville, Pennsylvania in 1903, Grange grew up in Wheaton, Illinois, where his family had moved when he was young. After high school—where he won 16 letters in four sports—he enrolled at the University of Illinois, where his exploits on the football field would gain him national recognition.

At UI, Grange became a terror on the gridiron. He was named to the All-American team three straight years (1923-1925). In his college career, he averaged 5.3 yards per carry, scored 31 touchdowns, and threw 6 scoring passes.

Red Grange

Grange's most sensational day at UI came in a game in 1924 versus the school's traditional rival, the University of Michigan; at the time, Michigan was unbeaten in 20 straight games. Grange rushed for 265 yards and 4 touchdowns—in the first 12 minutes of the game! In all, Grange scored five touchdowns the first five times he carried the ball, compiling 402 yards of total offense as Illinois rolled to victory, 39-14.

That game also saw Grange earn one of the most famous nicknames in sports history— the **Galloping Ghost**.

Grange left college immediately after his final game and joined the Chicago Bears of the NFL. His decision to play for the Bears before graduation day prompted a controversy that led to the adoption of the draft system, whereby a player had to graduate from college before he could sign with a pro team.

Despite missing several games with an injury and playing only briefly in others, Grange's time with the Bears was a great success. Unprecedented crowds came to games to watch Grange play, and he earned $100,000 — the highest salary a pro football player had made to that point. His presence gave the NFL sorely needed credibility, and greatly helped pro football gain widespread acceptance with the public.

Grange played two seasons with the New York Yankees in a newly formed American Football League after his initial season with the Bears, then returned to Chicago from 1929-34. In 1933, he took part in the NFL's first championship game, in which the Bears beat New York, 23-21.

After his playing days ended, Grange became an assistant coach, and later worked as a football announcer. In 1961, he retired to Florida, where he had business interests. He died of pneumonia on January 28, 1991.

With nearly 20 major championship single titles to her credit, **Helen Wills Moody** was one of the greatest female tennis players in the history of the sport.

She was born Helen Newington Wills in Centerville, California, and at her father's encouragement, she took up tennis as a youngster; she became a master of the game while she was still a teenager. She won the Pacific Coast Juniors at the age of 14 and the National Juniors at 15. In 1922, at the age of 16, she reached the finals of the U.S. Championships at Forest Hills. The following year, she defeated **Molla Mallory** to win the title.

Wills developed a devastatingly powerful forehand shot, which she used to dominate women's tennis during the 1920s and 1930s. She won a gold medal in both singles and doubles at the 1924 Olympic Games; she is the only American woman to win an Olympic gold medal at tennis.

Wills graduated from the University of California in 1927, and two years later, she married **Frederick S. Moody**; she competed throughout the next decade as Helen Wills Moody. The couple divorced in 1937, and in 1939, she married **Aidan Roark**.

During her career, Wills Moody was at her best in big tournaments. She won seven U.S. National singles championships; 1923-1925, 1927-1929, and 1931. She also won eight Wimbledon singles championships—1927-1930, 1932, 1933, 1935, and 1938—a record

that was not broken until 1990. Wills Moody also claimed four French singles titles,1928-1930, and 1932, and played in 10 Wightman Cup matches, winning 18 out of 20 singles contests.

Called **Little Miss Poker Face** because of her unemotional style of play, Wills Moody also became known for leading the bandwagon for more athletic attire for female tennis players. Instead of long, heavy skirts and long sleeves, her typical outfit on the court was a white sailor suit, white eyeshade, and white shoes and stockings.

In addition to her tennis career, Wills Moody was an author and an artist. Her autobiography, *Fifteen-Thirty: The Story of a Tennis Player*, was published in 1937, and she co-wrote a mystery, *Death Serves an Ace*, in 1939. Her drawings and paintings were displayed in several exhibitions in New York galleries.

Helen Wills Moody

(1911-1956) Track and Field, Golf

It is difficult to excel at one sport, let alone several. However, that is exactly what **Mildred "Babe" Didrikson-Zaharias** did, and that is why she was named the greatest woman athlete of the first half of the 20th century by the Associated Press in 1950.

Mildred Ella Didrikson was born in Port Arthur, Texas, in June of either 1911 or 1914, the year is in dispute; however, the official Babe Didrikson Zaharias Foundation, Inc. states the year as being 1911.

She was the daughter of a Norwegian ship carpenter, and as a girl she worked out with apparatus constructed from clotheslines and her mother's flatirons. She began making a name for herself in basketball. Then she hit multiple home runs in a baseball game, and soon she got the nickname Babe, after **Babe Ruth** (see no. 17).

As a teenager, Didrikson twice won a place on the All-American women's basketball team and set three national records in track and field. In 1932, she won the National Amateur Athletic Union track meet by winning five events and tying for first in a sixth. She was the sole member of the team for the Employers Casualty Company of Dallas; no one else was needed.

That same year in the Olympic Games, this woman who desired to "become the best athlete ever" set records in the javelin throw (143 feet, 4 inches) and the 80-meter hurdle (11.7 seconds) while winning gold medals in both

Babe Didrikson-Zaharias

events. She also won a silver medal in the high jump.

Having already conquered numerous sports, Didrikson took up golf in 1935. Displaying the single-minded determination that makes great athletes, she practiced her golf game 16 hours a day, driving an estimated 1,000 balls per day. Her average distance off the tee was 240 yards.

Once she began playing golf professionally, Didrikson was as good at that sport as she was at all the others she attempted. She won 82 amateur and professional tournaments, including the British Women's Open in 1947; she became the first American to ever win that tournament.

In 1937, she met professional wrestler **George Zaharias** on the golf course. They married the following year.

With exhibitions and championship wins, Didrikson-Zaharias earned in excess of $100,000 per year. She also wrote instructional articles for magazines and penned several books.

During her career on the links, she won every major women's golf championship, including the U.S. Amateur (1946), and three U.S. Open titles (1948, 1950, and 1954).

Her last U.S. Open victory in 1954 was even more remarkable because she had been diagnosed with cancer in 1953. Three years later, the disease claimed her life.

26. Sonja Henie
(1912-1969) Figure Skating

Sonja Henie changed the world of figure skating forever, turning a sport previously reserved for a few into one of widespread popularity.

Henie was born in Oslo, Norway, the second child of a fur merchant who indulged his children; she got her first pair of skates when she was eight years old. Henie quickly displayed so much ability on the ice that her father paid for the best skating instructions for her.

In 1923, at the age of ten, she won the Norwegian national championship. The following year, she competed in the Winter Olympics.

Henie was a natural athlete, good at many sports. She won the Scandinavian championships in tennis and skiing, and also excelled in horseback riding, sprinting, and swimming.

However, it was as a figure skater that Henie was destined to become internationally famous. In 1927, she won the first of ten consecutive world championships. One year later, she won her first Olympic gold medal. She would win two more, in 1932 and 1936. Overall, Henie won nearly 1,500 competitions throughout her career.

In 1936, Henie turned professional, and became the featured performer in a touring ice show. She continued skating in ice shows well into the 1950s.

Henie also signed a movie contract in Hollywood with **Darryl F. Zanuck**, who ran the 20th Century-Fox studio. The movies she made for Fox usually featured her skating, and were highly successful.

Henie's skill and the success of her films helped popularize the sport of competitive figure skating. Ice rinks sprung up throughout the Western Hemisphere, and a sport that had previously been the province of the rich or those in ice-bound countries suddenly was popular around the world. Ice dancing became a popular past time, and Henie's films inspired future Olympic champions like **Ludmila Beloussova** and **Oleg Protopopov** to don skates for the first time. (They won the gold medal in pairs skating in the 1964 and 1968 Olympics.)

Later in her career Henie made ice skating specials for television. When she died of leukemia in 1969, it was estimated that she had made approximately $47 million from all her various ventures. However, the money aside, she will forever be remembered as the person who brought figure skating "in from the cold."

Sonja Henie

Ben Hogan

Born the son of a blacksmith in Dublin, Texas, **Ben Hogan** rose up from an extremely poor background to become one of the greatest golfers of all time.

After his father died when Hogan was ten, he had to sell newspapers to help keep the family fed. When he was 12, Hogan switched to caddying at the Glen Garden Country Club in Fort Worth, and his career on the links was underway.

Hogan became a professional in 1931, and it took him several years to establish himself. However, by the early 1940s, he began to dominate the American golf scene; he was the leading money winner on the tour from 1940 to 1942.

He became known as a superb shot-maker, dubbed **the Hawk** by his competitors. Golfing great **Gene Sarazen** once said, "From tee to green, there never was anyone to compare with Hogan. If he had been able to putt as well as **Bobby Jones** (see no. 21) or **Jack Nicklaus** (see no. 58), no one could have come close to him. Yet he was such a superb shot maker that his putting was never put to too severe a test."

After he served in the Army Air Corps during World War II, Hogan rejoined the tour in 1945, and won 35 tournaments in the next 4 1/2 years.

However, in February 1949, tragedy struck. Hogan and his wife were driving home to Fort Worth when a huge bus went out of control and careened into their lane. Instinctively, Hogan threw himself across the seat to protect his wife. His heroic action worked, as she suffered only minor injuries. But Hogan sustained a double fracture of the pelvis, a broken collarbone, a broken left ankle, and a broken rib.

It was feared that Hogan would have difficulty walking again. But the people who made that prediction had not counted on Hogan's iron will and determination. In January 1950, less than one year after the accident, Hogan battled **Sammy Snead** into a playoff in the Los Angeles Open. A few months later he won the U.S. Open title.

Nine months after his U.S. Open victory Hogan won the 1951 Masters Tournament, and then won the U.S. Open again. In 1953 he won the Masters, U.S. Open, and the British Open for a near-grand slam. All together, from 1946 to 1953, Hogan won four U.S. Opens, two Masters, two PGA tournaments, and the only British Open in which he ever competed.

Hogan was named Professional Golfers Association (PGA) Player of the Year four times. After his retirement, he started a golf manufacturing company that bore his name.

28. Jesse Owens
(1913-1980) Track and Field

Jesse Owens will always be remembered for more than winning four gold medals at the 1936 Olympics. His name resonates throughout history because he accomplished that feat under the disdainful eyes of a man who had called all members of Owens's race "inferior," the German dictator, **Adolf Hitler**.

Owens was born James Cleveland "JC" Owens in Danville, Alabama. When he was nine, his family moved to Cleveland, Ohio. Owens ran in his first meet when he was 13, and by the time he was in high school, he was a nationally known sprinter. After graduation, he enrolled at Ohio State University, paying his way by working as a night elevator operator.

Owens's first Big Ten track meet was held on May 25, 1935. On that day, Owens gave an incredible performance. He tied the world record for the 100-yard dash (9.4 seconds); set a new world record for the broad jump (26' 8 1/4"); set a new world record for the 220-yard dash (20.3 seconds); and set a new world record for the 220-yard low hurdles (22.6 seconds).

After that day, Owens's fame in track and field was assured. As it turned out, his future accomplishments guaranteed that his name would join the very short list of sports' immortal figures.

The 1936 Olympics were held in Berlin, Germany, and Nazi leader Adolf Hitler believed that the games were the perfect forum for his theories that the Aryan race was superior to all others. The Nazis ridiculed the United States for having African-Americans—who Hitler claimed were "inferior" people— on its team. However, when the Olympics were over, Hitler was the one subject to ridicule and humiliation—

black American athletes won six gold medals, led in force by Jesse Owens.

Under tremendous pressure, Owens was simply outstanding. He won the 100-meter dash, the 200-meter dash, and the broad jump. In so doing, he broke two Olympic records and nearly broke a third. In addition, he led the American relay team that won the 400-meter relay in 39.8 seconds— a new world record. A grim-faced Hitler left the Olympic stadium before Owens was awarded his third gold medal.

Sadly, while Owens had great success on the international stage, he found it very difficult to earn a living when he returned home. At the time, many opportunities were still closed to African-Americans within the United States.

However, Owens was as determined away from the field of athletic competition as he was on it. He eventually began his own business and for years ran a successful public relations firm. In 1976, he was awarded the **Presidential Medal of Freedom**, the nation's highest civilian honor.

Jesse Owens

29. Willie Mosconi
(1913-1993) Pocket Billiards

Willie Mosconi dominated the sport of pocket billiards in a way no one ever has before—or since. He is probably the greatest 14-1 straight pool champion the sport has ever known.

Born in Philadelphia in 1913, Mosconi was a child prodigy at billiards. His father owned a billiards parlor, but wouldn't let his son play; so, Mosconi would sneak in at night when he was five years old and practice with a broomstick and potatoes. Surprisingly, he then put down his cue stick and did not take it up again until 1931. Once he did, he established supremacy over the game.

Willie Mosconi

Mosconi entered his first major tournament in 1937, and won his first world pocket billiards championship in 1941. He was champion again in 1942, and then from 1944-1948, and 1950-1955. When he retired from competition in 1957 after suffering a stroke, he still held the title.

During his career, Mosconi established a number of records, including exhibition high run, 527 balls; high run during a game, 127; high run in tournament play, 150; and most consecutive games won in tournament play, 14.

Beginning in the 1950s, Mosconi began giving numerous public exhibitions that helped popularize the game of billiards. In 1954, he wrote a book, *Willie Mosconi on Pocket Billiards*, that further helped bring the game out of the dank back rooms of bars and poolrooms and into the mainstream of American life. Over the years, he also was a willing advisor to many youthful contenders in the sport. With his impeccably dressed look and his near-scholarly attitude about the game, Mosconi established an image of the pocket billiards champion as a figure of considerable finesse and skill—and class.

Mosconi served as a technical advisor to the 1961 Paul Newman-Jackie Gleason movie, *The Hustler*, a film that made the name of pool shark **Minnesota Fats** (Rudolph Walderone) a household word. In 1978, Mosconi and "Fats" played an exhibition match featured on television; Mosconi easily won.

Mosconi died of a heart attack in Haddon Heights, New Jersey in 1993.

Known as the **Brown Bomber** for the way he bombarded his opponents in the ring, **Joe Louis** was a great and memorable heavyweight champion.

He was born Joseph Louis Barrow near Lafayette, Alabama. He did odd jobs as a teenager and attended Bronson Vocational School before deciding he wanted to be a prizefighter.

Louis lost his first amateur bout, but quickly proved to be a formidable opponent in the ring. In 1934, he won the Amateur Athletic Union Light Heavyweight championship. He went on to record 43 knockout victories in 54 fights as an amateur.

Turning pro, Louis won his initial fight by a first-round knockout on July 4, 1934 over an opponent named **Jack Kraken**. Louis had 25 more fights in 1934-35, beating such prominent heavyweights as former champions **Primo Carnera** and **Max Baer**.

One fight Louis lost, however, was in 1936 against German fighter **Max Schmeling**. It was a defeat that Nazi dictator **Adolf Hitler** gloated over, claiming more evidence of his philosophy of Aryan "racial superiority."

By the time Louis fought Schmeling in a rematch in 1938, the Brown Bomber had become the heavyweight champ by virtue of a victory over **James J. Braddock**. In front of a roaring crowd of 70,000 fans at Yankee Stadium in New York, and millions more listening to the radio broadcast, Louis hammered Schmeling, knocking him out in just over two minutes of the first round. The fight made Louis a national hero, as many considered it a victory for democracy over Nazism and Hitler's repulsive racial theories.

As champion, Louis beat any and all comers, fighting so often in 1940-41 that his opponents came to be known as the "Bum of the Month" club. He was not deterred by either a faster man or a harder puncher, and

Joe Louis

successfully defended his title 30 times over an 11-year period, from the late 30s to the late 40s. "He can run, but he can't hide," Louis said about one opponent, and it turned out to be true of everyone he fought.

Louis joined the army in 1942 and spent three years staging boxing exhibitions for U.S. soldiers, traveling some 21,000 miles to entertain troops.

Louis retired as the undefeated heavyweight champion in 1949. The following year he returned to the ring, but the old magic was gone. He lost twice, including once by knockout at the hands of **Rocky Marciano** (see no. 37). Louis then permanently retired with a professional record of 68 wins—54 by knockout—and 3 losses.

Despite some financial problems with the government in his later years, Louis retained his great popularity with the public until his death on April 12, 1981.

Joe DiMaggio
(1914-1999) Baseball

With his flawless grace in the field and near-perfect swing at the plate, **Joe DiMaggio** was one of the greatest baseball players of all-time.

Born in 1914, in Martinez, California, DiMaggio grew up in San Francisco as a baseball-loving teenager. He was so skilled that he signed with the minor league San Francisco Seals when he was just 17 years old.

In 1933, DiMaggio hit .340 and batted safely in 61 games for the Seals, causing major league scouts to start gathering on his doorstep. However, then he suffered a freak knee injury in January, 1935, that caused most of those same scouts to consider him "damaged goods" and lose interest. The New York Yankees were one team that kept after DiMaggio, however, and as a result of the injury they were able to sign him for a low $25,000.

When DiMaggio came up to the big leagues in 1936, the Yankees were a team in transition. **Babe Ruth** was gone, and even though they had slugging first baseman **Lou Gehrig**, he was already past his prime. The team was searching for a new leader, and DiMaggio quickly became that player. He hit .323 in his first season with 29 homers, and helped the Yanks win the first of four consecutive World Series titles.

DiMaggio quickly became the most recognizable player on a team of champions, always playing hard and playing to win. He once said that he played hard every day because he never knew when there might be someone in the stands who was seeing him for the first time. Overall, he led the Yankees to 10 pennants in his 13 seasons.

In 1941, DiMaggio set what many people feel is the one unbreakable record in baseball: he hit safely in 56 straight games, a period of over two months. He recorded 91 hits, 15 homers, and a .408 batting average during that period.

DiMaggio was a three-time winner of the Most Valuable Player Award (1939, 1941, and 1947). His lifetime batting average was .325. Surprisingly, for a power hitter of his caliber, he rarely struck out. He notched 361 home runs and struck out only 369 times during his career.

In the field DiMaggio was a master of making every catch look easy. He was recognized as one of the most superb center fielders in the game's history.

Inevitably, age and injuries took their toll, and DiMaggio retired after the 1951 season. In the 1950s, he was married briefly to famed actress **Marilyn Monroe**. His later work on television commercials and appearances at old timer's games kept him in the public eye for many years.

Joe DiMaggio

Marion Ladewig is considered by many people to be the greatest female bowler of all time.

Ladewig was born in Grand Rapids, Michigan in 1914. She began competing on the lanes as a young woman in her early twenties, long before the existence of a woman's professional bowling tour. However, Ladewig was lucky; the Michigan area where she grew up was home to some of the most competitive bowling in the country at that time. Ladewig fit right in; soon, however, she would eclipse everyone she played against.

In 1944-45, Ladewig had the highest bowling average in the United States; it was a distinction she would earn three more times. In 1949, she became the first person to win the Bowling Proprietor's Association of America (BPAA) Woman's All-Star title. (It is now called the Women's U.S. Open.)

Then in 1950, Ladewig had one of the most spectacular years of any bowler in history. She won the Women's International Bowling Congress (WIBC) all-events title on the national level. She also won all-events titles on the city and state levels—becoming the only bowler in history to sweep the sport in such a manner.

As the years rolled on, so did Ladewig, often in spectacular fashion. In 1951, she maintained an eight day average of 247.5. In 1955, she won the WIBC's all-events and doubles championships.

Ladewig has sometimes been compared to titans of other sports, such as **Babe Ruth** (see no. 17) and **Gordie Howe** (see no. 41), and she certainly had the accomplishments to back up that comparison. She won the BPAA All-Star tournament eight times and the World Invitational title five times. She was a nine-time winner of the Bowling Writers Association of America Woman Bowler of the Year award —she won it more than twice as often as any other woman in history.

Ladewig's popularity was such that she helped give rise to the Professional Women's Bowling Association. At the group's first professional tournament in 1960, Ladewig emerged victorious.

Marion Ladewig

Ladewig placed third in the Associated Press's 1963 Woman Athlete of the Year poll. It was the first time that a bowler had ever made it that close to the top.

In 1964, Ladewig was inducted into the WIBC Hall of Fame. She retired in 1965, but still remained a force in the game by working as an advisor to bowling equipment manufacturer, the Brunswick Corporation.

Many baseball experts simply call **Theodore Samuel "Ted" Williams** the greatest hitter who ever played the game.

He was born in San Diego, California, and in his boyhood he would often practice swinging an imaginary bat at imaginary baseballs in his backyard. When he was just 17 years old, Williams signed with the minor league San Diego Padres.

Two years later, he was signed by the Boston Red Sox of the American League. When he reported to spring training with the Sox in 1938, his unbelievably brash attitude earned him a quick trip back to the minors. Determined to prove that he belonged in the big leagues, Williams tore up the American Association that year, hitting .366 with 43 homers and 142 RBI. Those totals were enough to win the league's Triple Crown, and also convinced the Red Sox to recall him to the majors.

Ted Williams

In his rookie season with Boston, Williams blistered the ball at a .327 clip, with 31 homers and a league leading 145 runs batted in. However, that was nothing compared to the 1941 season, when Williams hit .406—the last player to hit .400 or better in the 20th century. Williams began the last day of the season hitting .3995; he could have sat out the final day's doubleheader and been recognized with an official average of .400. However, true to his competitive nature, he played both contests, going six for eight to firmly boost his average above the .400 mark. He wanted to make sure that no one could say that Ted Williams hadn't legitimately earned that historic mark.

Williams went on to have a brilliant career—spent entirely with the Red Sox. He won six batting titles, two Triple Crowns, and was a two-time Most Valuable Player. When he retired after the 1960 season, he had a .344 lifetime average, with 521 home runs and .483 on-base average— the highest in baseball history.

During his career, Williams lost nearly six full seasons to service in the military— first in World War II, and then again during the Korean War. No one knows what his final lifetime totals would have been had he not lost those years to military duty.

Perhaps his only disappointment on the diamond was in the World Series. He led the Red Sox to the World Series only once, in 1946, where they lost to the St. Louis Cardinals.

After his retirement, Williams remained connected to the game for the rest of his life. He managed for a while—unsuccessfully— and then tutored and advised many young hitters as they made their way through the major leagues.

34. Patty Berg
(1918-) Golf

Interested in sports from when she was just a child, **Patty Berg** grew up to become one of the leading female golfers of her era.

Born in Minneapolis, Minnesota in 1918, Berg showed an affinity for sports as a teenager—only it wasn't golf, but football! She was the quarterback of the 50th Street Tigers, which—except for her—was an all-boys team. Her parents, deciding that she was too old to be involved in such activities, pointed her toward golf at the age of 14. They bought her a membership at the Interlachen Country Club. One year later, she won the Minneapolis city championship, and her amateur career was launched.

As an amateur, Berg was the Minnesota state champion and won 29 titles in 7 years, including the 1938 U.S. Amateur title. She became widely recognized as the best, and most famous, female golfer in the United States.

It was inevitable that Berg would turn pro, which she did in 1940. Since there was no women's professional tour at the time, she earned a living by giving clinics and exhibitions. In 1941, she had a serious automobile accident, and was sidelined for more than a year.

When she returned to the game, Berg won the 1943 Western Open and All-American at Tam O'Shanter. She then joined the Marines. When she got out of the service, she won the 1946 U.S. Women's Open. She then became one of the founders of the Ladies Professional Golf Association (LPGA), and served as its first president from 1948-1952.

During the years from 1949-1960, Berg won 39 LPGA tournaments. She was the leading money winner among women golfers in 1954, 1955, and 1957. She was also a three-time winner (1953, 1955, and 1956) of the Vare Trophy for the lowest average round, and was also named Female Athlete of the Year by the Associated Press three times (1938, 1943, and 1955). In 1952, she shot an LPGA 18-hole record of 64. Throughout her career, Berg qualified for every tournament she ever entered—a record she still holds.

In 1951, when she was inducted into the LPGA Hall of Fame, Berg said, "I'm very happy that I gave up football, or I wouldn't be here tonight." A legion of golfing fans are just as happy.

Patty Berg

35. Jackie Robinson
(1919-1972) Baseball

Jackie Robinson

As major league baseball's first African-American player, **Jackie Robinson** proved his greatness on the field—and off it.

Although he was born in Cairo, Georgia, Robinson grew up in Pasadena, California, where he became a multi-sport star in high school. When he attended UCLA, Robinson continued to shine on the athletic fields. Ironically, it was for football, not baseball, that Robinson left school in 1941, signing to play with the NFL's professional team, the Los Angeles Bulldogs.

Military service interrupted Robinson's dreams of gridiron glory. By the time he got out of the military, his career focus had shifted from football to baseball. He signed with the Kansas City Monarchs, one of the elite teams of baseball's Negro Leagues.

By the mid-1940s, the American sports world was changing. Buoyed by their push for equal opportunity status in World War II, African-Americans were also pushing hard to end inequities in all walks of life, including sports. Baseball was America's national pastime and number one sport, and with its notorious "color line," it stood out so shockingly in its refusal to let blacks participate.

Robinson was not the best player in the Negro Leagues, but he was the one that **Branch Rickey** of the Brooklyn Dodgers thought would be able to break the color line with class and dignity. Rickey knew that the first African-American to play in the majors would be subject to torrents of verbal abuse, and he needed someone who would endure all that mindless anger with extraordinary good grace. In Robinson, he found his man.

Rickey signed Robinson to a professional contract, and after one minor league season in 1946, Robinson came up to the Dodgers.

The racial bigotry and abuse that Robinson faced was almost beyond comprehension, but somehow he survived, and answered his critics with his on-field play. In his first season, Robinson's skill and electrifying speed netted him the National League's Rookie-of-the-Year Award. He hit .297 and led the league with 29 stolen bases. Two years later, he hit .342 to win the league's batting title and Most Valuable Player Award. He brought the running, go-for-broke style of the Negro Leagues back to the majors, and it helped re-energize the game.

Robinson did not have a long career, perhaps because the strain of all the racism he faced wore him down. He retired after the 1956 season, having sparked the Dodgers to six pennants and one World Series title during his time with them. He was inducted into the Hall of Fame in 1962.

36. John Davis
(1921-1984) Weightlifting

The first African-American to win an Olympic weightlifting championship, **John Davis** in his prime was known as the **Strongest Man in the World.**

Born in Brooklyn, New York in 1921, Davis displayed his tremendous strength when he was young. At the age of 17, he won the light heavyweight world championship in Vienna. He then began an amazing streak in which he was undefeated in all competitions between 1938 and 1953. During this time, he broke 19 world records, won 12 national titles and a gold medal at the Pan-American Games.

In 1941, before middle heavyweight became an officially recognized weight class, Davis completed lifts of 322.25 pounds in the press, 317.5 pounds in the snatch, and a clean

and jerk of 370 pounds. This added up to the extraordinary total of 1009.75 pounds. Davis went on to become a full-fledged heavyweight. His best individual lifts were 342 pounds in the press, 330.5 pounds in the snatch, and 402 pounds in the clean and jerk. Davis could curl 215 pounds and bench press 425. He once performed a two-handed dead lift of 705 pounds.

Davis is one of only 12 weightlifters to have won two Olympic championships. At the 1948 Olympics, Davis lifted 137.5 kg in the press and snatch, and 177 kg. in the jerk, for a total of 314.5 kg. He returned to the Games in 1952 in Helsinki, Finland, and lifted a total of 460 kg: 150 in the press, 145 in the snatch, and 165 in the jerk.

Davis was the world champion six times at his weight classification, and from 1948 - 1956, he won 32 state, national, Olympic and world weightlifting championships. He was the world's amateur heavyweight champion in 1946, 1947, 1949, 1950, and 1951.

In 1952, Davis was the subject of the first Olympic-related film made by noted sports filmmaker **Bud Greenspan**. It was called, appropriately enough, *The Strongest Man in the World.*

Davis's last appearance on the lifting platform was not a happy one. During the 1956 Olympic trials, he tore a ligament in his knee attempting to clean nearly 400 pounds and had to be carried off the stage on a stretcher.

In an age when African-American athletes were struggling for recognition, John Davis helped greatly raise their visibility.

Rocky Marciano

Rocky Marciano, the "**Brockton Blockbuster,**" was one of the greatest heavyweight champions of all time. Flinging the thunderous right hook he called Susie Q, Marciano compiled a record of 49-0, retiring as the only undefeated heavyweight champion in boxing history.

Born Rocco Francis Marchegiano in Brockton, Massachusetts, he began fighting in the U.S. Army when he was 20 years old. After he got out, he continued fighting under an assumed name, **Rocky Mack,** to preserve his amateur status. He won all of his amateur fights except one.

When Marciano turned professional in 1947, he quickly proved that he was going to be a force—only two of his first nine opponents lasted beyond the first round. He was a paradox in many ways, savagely pummeling his opponents on one hand, and then feeling bad about winning the bout. In 1951, after pounding former champion **Joe Louis,**

Marciano wept, and later sent the ex-champ a note telling him how sorry he was that the fight had turned out the way it did. When a boxer named **Carmine Vingo** was left paralyzed from the waist down after a fight with Marciano, Rocky paid the $2,000 for his hospital bills.

With his straight-ahead, relentless pounding style, Marciano faced technical wizard **Jersey Joe Walcott** for the heavyweight title in September, 1952. Walcott knocked Marciano down in the first round, and for two full rounds he was blinded by medication that had been put on one of his facial cuts. Yet Marciano survived, and in the 13th round he landed his devastating right hook and knocked Walcott out.

Marciano went on to defend his title five more times over the next several years, including a first round knockout of Walcott in their rematch and two defeats of former champion **Ezzard Charles**. One fight with Charles went 15 rounds—the only 15-round fight of Marciano's career.

On September 21, 1955, Marciano met light-heavyweight champion **Archie Moore** in a fight that has been called one of the greatest bouts in boxing history.

The two men often stood toe-to-toe in the ring, throwing punches at each other with wild abandon, all semblance of strategy or style forgotten. Finally Marciano KO'd the still-game but exhausted Moore in the ninth round.

It was Marciano's last fight. He retired in April, 1956, partly at the urging of his mother. In 1969, he participated in a series of fight sequences with **Muhammad Ali** (see no. 62) that were fed into a computer to determine the greatest heavyweight of all time. Marciano won by a 13th-round knockout.

Marciano died on August 31, 1969, when the light plane he was traveling in crashed.

38. George Mikan
(1924-) Basketball

Professional basketball's first superstar, **George Mikan** was the first dominant big man in the National Basketball Association. Although his time in the league was relatively brief, he left a lasting impact on the game, and his career would foreshadow the later emergence of great NBA centers such as **Bill Russell** (see no. 51) and **Wilt Chamberlain** (see no. 54).

George Mikan was born in 1924, in Joliet, Illinois. He didn't play basketball in high school because he was awkward, and a badly broken leg kept him recovering at home for a year and a half. In 1942, he entered DePaul University in Chicago, as a 6 foot, 10 inch 245 pound freshman who wore thick glasses.

At DePaul, under the coaching of **Ray Meyer**, Mikan not only learned the game of basketball—he became a great player. Meyer taught Mikan the fundamentals, as well as how to make hook shots with either hand. In three years, Mikan was a three-time All-American (1944-1946), and college player of the year in 1945 and 1946. He also led DePaul to the 1945 National Invitational Tournament title.

After school, Mikan joined the professional Chicago American Gears of the National Basketball League. He led the Gears to the NBL championship in 1947, and after the Gears folded, Mikan joined the NBL's Minneapolis Lakers, with whom he was to reach stardom.

In 1948, the NBL and the Basketball Association of America merged to form the National Basketball Association (NBA). Mikan led the new league in scoring its first three years, and led the Lakers to five league championships—1949, 1950, 1952-1954— in six years. He was such a dominant player that he was sometimes guarded by two and even three defenders.

During his career Mikan was named to the All-Star team six consecutive seasons, averaged 22.6 points per game, and scored 11,764 points in 520 games; his average in post-season play was 23.5.

Mikan was such a dominating force in the sport that in 1950 the Associated Press voted him the Greatest Basketball Player of the first half of the 20th Century.

Mikan retired after the 1956 season, then came back to coach the Lakers for one year. When the American Basketball Association was formed in 1967 he became its first commissioner, a position he held until he resigned in 1969. As commissioner, Mikan came up with the unique idea of the league's red, white, and blue multi-colored ball.

Mikan was part of the first class elected to the basketball Hall of Fame in 1959. In 1996, he was named one of the NBA's 50 greatest players as selected for the league's 50th Anniversary Team.

George Mikan

39. Don Carter
(1926-) Bowling

With great skill and tireless promotion of his sport, **Don Carter** indeed lived up to his nickname, **"Mr. Bowling."**

Born on July 29, 1926 in St. Louis, Missouri, Carter was a two-sports star in high school, but neither one was bowling. Baseball and football were his stand-out sports. Carter entered the U.S. Navy during World War II, and after being discharged, he played one season of minor league baseball as a pitcher and infielder. He then returned to St. Louis to manage a bowling center.

Once the man and the sport finally met, Carter quickly established his mastery over the game of bowling. He won the Bowling Proprietors' Association of America All-Star Tournament (today, the BPAA U.S. Open) for the first time in 1953. He would go on to win it three more times—1954, 1957, and 1958. The Professional Bowlers Association (PBA) was formed in 1958, and Carter won the group's first championship tournament in 1960 with a score of 6,512 for 30 games. The following year, he won the American Bowling Congress (ABC) Masters Tournament with an average score of 211.18.

Carter was voted Bowler of the Year six times—in 1953, 1954, 1957, 1958, 1960, and 1962. That year he led the PBAA tour in earnings with $22,525, and in overall average with a score of 212.84.

Carter led the PBAA in earnings again with $49,972 in 1964.

In 1970, a poll named him the best bowler of all time. He is a member of the Hall of Fame of both the ABC and PBA.

Don Carter

Bob Cousy was known for his phenomenal playmaking ability, which revolutionized basketball. He also was a big part of the fabled Boston Celtics dynasty of the late 1950s and 1960s.

The son of French immigrants, Robert Joseph Cousy was born in New York City in 1928, and spoke only French until he was six years old. His family moved to St. Albans, Queens, when he was 12, and when he was in junior high school he began experimenting with ball-handling—behind-the-back passes and other techniques that would fool the opposition. Cousy didn't make the junior varsity squad in high school until his sophomore year, and in his junior year he wasn't allowed to play until January. Nevertheless, in a full senior year season, he led the city in scoring and was named to the All-City team.

Cousy attended Holy Cross College on a basketball scholarship. As a freshman, he played on an NCAA championship team and was an All-American in his senior year. Nicknamed the **Houdini of the Hardwood**, his brilliant ball handling influenced the entire team.

Ironically, although Cousy is identified with the Boston Celtics, they initially passed up the chance to draft him. He was taken instead by the Tri-Cities Blackhawks, and then went to the Chicago American Gears.

When the Gears folded, Cousy's name was put into a hat, along with those of a few teammates. The Celtics picked him out, and years later legendary coach **Red Auerbach** marveled, "We got stuck with the greatest player in the league when we drew his name out of a hat."

In his 13 seasons with the Celtics, (1950-1963) Cousy helped them win six NBA championships—1957, and consecutively from 1959 through 1963. Teaming with defensive genius **Bill Russell** (see no. 51),

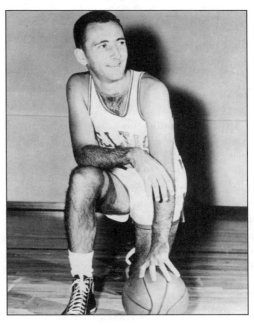

Bob Cousy

Cousy helped build the Celtics into one of the true dynasties in professional sports.

Individually, Cousy led the league in assists eight times, and was chosen for the NBA All-Star team every season he was with the Celtics. In a 1953 playoff game, Cousy made 10 field goals and a playoff record 30 of 32 free throws, for a total of 50 points. He was named the league's Most Valuable Player in 1957, the first time the Celtics won the championship.

Cousy retired after the 1963 season at the age of 34, leaving Russell and others to continue the Celtics' winning tradition. When he quit, Cousy ranked first in the league in career assists and third in scoring.

After his retirement, Cousy coached at Boston College for six seasons, and then coached the NBA's Cincinnati Royals (later the Kansas City-Omaha Kings) for several seasons.

41. Gordie Howe
(1928-) Hockey

Gordie Howe's nickname says it all: **"Mr. Hockey."** In a career that spanned more than 30 years, Howe set numerous National Hockey League scoring records and was named the league's Most Valuable Player 6 times.

Howe was born in Floral, Saskatchewan, Canada; his family soon moved to nearby Saskatoon, where Howe learned to play hockey on a skating rink in the family backyard, substituting a tennis ball for a puck.

He was so proficient at the game that by the time he was 15, he was already being pursued by teams from the NHL. At 16, he was signed by the Detroit Red Wings, who sent him to the minor leagues.

When he was 18, Howe joined the Red Wings, where he played steady but unspectacular hockey for the first three sea-

Gordie Howe

sons. However, in the 1949 Stanley Cup play-offs, he notched eight goals and three assists—a total unmatched by any other player that year.

That series seemed to ignite something in Howe. He went on to lead the NHL in scoring four straight years—1951-1954—and six times overall. With his matchless stick-handling and shooting from either side of his body, few could keep up with him. In addition to being a prolific scorer, Howe was an outstanding defensive player who averaged nearly twice the playing time on the ice of most forwards.

Howe was an ageless wonder who seemed as if he might play hockey forever. On his 25th anniversary with the Red Wings, NHL coaches named him "The smartest player, best passer, best playmaker and best puck carrier" in the league. By that time, Howe's sons Mark and Marty were also playing for Detroit.

Shortly thereafter, though, the Red Wings made the mistake of taking Howe off the ice and putting him in a front-office job. Howe and his sons quickly departed for the Houston club of the new World Hockey Association (WHA). He led Houston to the league championship in 1972, proving that there was plenty of life left in his hockey legs.

Howe won the WHA's MVP Award in 1974 and led Houston to another championship in 1975. He and his sons then signed with the WHA's Hartford Whalers; the Whalers joined the NHL in 1977, and Howe continued to play for them until he finally retired in 1980 at the remarkable age of 52.

When Howe retired, he was the NHL leader in career goals scored and total points. He is now second to **Wayne Gretzky** (see no. 90) in both categories. Howe also ranks among the career leaders in Stanley Cup playoff goals, assists, and points.

Jacques Plante
(1929-1986) Hockey

The pillar of the Montreal Canadien dynasty in the late 1950s, and the first goalie to wear a protective mask, **Jacques Plante** significantly influenced the sport of hockey.

Plante was an asthmatic child in Mont-Carmel, Quebec, Canada who began playing hockey as a young boy. He became so good that by age 20, he was a prominent minor league player for the Montreal Royals. He got his big break in the 1953 Stanley Cup semifinals, when the Montreal Canadiens needed him to replace their regular goaltender. Plante sparkled in net for the two games he played, allowing just one goal and leading Montreal to the finals. In that series, he split the goaltending duties with the regular goalie as the Canadiens beat the Boston Bruins to win the Stanley Cup.

Installed the following season as the Canadiens' regular goalie, Plante rapidly established himself as the National Hockey League's leading net-keeper. He led the NHL in shutouts three straight years (1956-1958) and in goals-against average from 1956-1960 and again in 1962. During that time the Canadiens won five straight Stanley Cups (1956-1960). Plante was voted the NHL's Most Valuable Player in 1961.

Plante was an innovator in the crease. He developed the now-common technique of moving out of the goal area with the puck still in play in order to stop a rush by the other team or to break up their play. Conversely, he was not shy about moving out of the crease to aid his own team's efforts.

However, his biggest innovation came when he began wearing a molded plastic mask to protect himself; he began that practice after he was injured in the face by a rocketing puck. While goalies had worn plastic masks to protect themselves during practices, Plante was the first to do so during games. Soon all goalies were doing the same to protect themselves from the hard rubber pucks.

Plante retired in 1965, but came back with the St. Louis Blues in 1967. Proving that age hadn't diminished his skills, he once again led the NHL in goals-against average in the 1967-68 season.

After several seasons in the World Hockey Association, Plante finally retired for good in 1975, at the age of 45. He finished his career as a seven-time winner of the Goaltender of the Year Award, with 82 shutouts and a 2.38 goals-against average. In 1978, he was elected to the NHL Hall of Fame.

Jacques Plante

43. **Roger Bannister**
(1929-) Track and Field

Sometimes sports heroes and star athletes are the most unlikely of people. That is certainly the case with Sir **Roger Bannister**, a mild-mannered English medical student who became the first man in history to run a mile in less than four minutes.

For hundreds of years, it was considered impossible to run a mile in under four minutes. Even the greatest runners in the history of the sport, such as **Paavo Nurmi** (see no. 20), couldn't break the four-minute barrier. However, in 1952, Australian runner **John Landy** made it known that the four-minute mile was his goal. He came close, clocking a time of 4:02.

Roger Bannister

At the same time, Roger Bannister was studying Landy's runs, convinced that he could do better.

Bannister was born in Harrow, England, and was educated at Oxford. As a runner, he had much in common with Nurmi. Like that great track star, Bannister believed that he could better his time by intensive training, combined with a careful analysis of running conditions, pacing, timed acceleration, and other factors. He knew that he would have to run four laps averaging slightly less than 60 seconds each to shatter the 4-minute barrier.

In May, 1953, after intensive training, he put his theory to the test. He ran the first two laps too slowly, but still set a new British mile record of 4:03.6.

When Landy subsequently ran a 4:02 mile and declared that he had hit "a brick wall," Bannister knew that the 4-minute record was his for the taking. He stepped up his training from December 1953 through the spring of 1954. He circled May 6, 1954 on his calendar. On that date, Oxford would have a meet with the British Amateur Athletic Association. He determined to go for the record at that event.

Bannister trained rigorously for weeks before the meet, then stopped training a few days before to conserve his energy. When the big day came, Bannister ran the first quarter in 57.5 seconds, and at the half-mile, he was at 1:58. His three-quarters time was 3:00.5, and he broke the tape at 3:59.4 —a new world record.

Just over a month later, Landy beat Bannister's mark, clocking a 3:58 mile. In June, 1954, the two men competed against each other at the British Commonwealth Games. Ironically, both men recorded times of less than four minutes, although neither set a world record; Bannister won the race.

Bannister's last win in international competition was in the 1,500-meter race in the European games later in 1954. He subsequently retired from running to practice medicine. He was knighted in 1975.

44. **Arnold Palmer**
(1929-) Golf

Arnold Palmer came along just as televised sports were growing in popularity, and golf in particular was reaching a greater audience than ever before. The face of golf on television became the face of the personable and talented Palmer, who became the first golfer to earn more than $1 million in prize money.

Palmer was born in Latrobe, Pennsylvania, to a father who was a greens keeper and pro at the local golf course. Showing an early interest in the game, Palmer began playing golf when he was 3 years old, and became a caddie at the age of 11. In 1946, he entered his first national golf tournament when he was 17.

Then his career was interrupted by tragedy. His best friend was killed in an automobile accident, and a distraught Palmer joined the Coast Guard. When he was discharged in 1953, he became a sales representative.

Arnold Palmer

However, he couldn't abandon golf. In 1954, he won the National Amateur Championship, and made a life-altering decision: he decided to turn pro. For several years he and his wife scrambled to survive financially, but the Palmer income grew as his golf game improved. In 1958, he led the PGA with $42,607 in winnings.

Palmer was at his best in big tournaments. He won four Masters championships—in

1958, 1960, 1962, and 1964—and the British Open twice, in 1961 and 1962. Sometimes his victories came in spectacular fashion. In 1960, he was 14th going into the final round at the U.S. Open. He birdied 6 of the first 7 holes, posted a record-tying tournament score of 30 for the first nine holes, and finished the second nine with 35. His 65 was the lowest final round ever shot by a U.S. Open winner up to that time.

In 1963, Palmer won more than $125,000, and by 1968 he had become the first golfer to earn more than $1 million in prize money. However, Palmer not only won a lot of tournaments and prize money; he is credited with almost single-handedly popularizing golf during the 1960s. With his large fan following known as "Arnie's Army," and his "everyman" demeanor, he brought golf into the television age, and introduced the game to a whole legion of at-home viewers.

In 1980, Palmer joined the senior tour, and immediately won the Seniors Championship that year; he won it again in 1984. Throughout he 1980s, he continued his winning ways on the senior tour.

With his various business interests, Palmer remained before the public well after he retired from the game. To millions of people, he'll always be the face of professional golf.

Pat McCormick
(1930-) Diving

A member of the U.S. Olympic Hall of Fame, **Pat McCormick** is the only female diver to win two gold medals in two consecutive Olympics.

Pat McCormick

Born Patricia Keller in 1930 in Seal Beach, California, she took to the water at an early age. She won the Long Beach One-Meter Gold Cup at the age of 14. After graduating high school, she attended California State University at Long Beach. In 1949, she married Glenn McCormick.

McCormick won her first national championship at the national outdoor platform dive in 1949. She won the same event four more times—1950, 1951, 1954, and 1955. She also won the outdoor 1-meter and 3-meter springboard championships six times, in 1950, 1951, and from 1953-1956.

McCormick was just as dominant indoors. She won the 1-meter springboard five straight years beginning in 1951, and the 3-meter in 1951, 1952, 1954, 1955.

McCormick first gained international

recognition in 1951 by winning the 10-meter platform event at the Pan-American Games. However, it was in the following year that the world really took notice—she won gold medals in both the springboard and platform events at the 1952 Summer Olympics in Helsinki, Finland.

McCormick continued her international success at the 1955 Pan-American Games, winning the springboard and platform events. The following year she gave birth to a son; however, she showed that childbirth had not affected her athletic skills. Eight months later, she won gold medals again in both the springboard and platform events at the 1956 Olympics in Melbourne, Australia, becoming the first diver to win both events in two Olympics.

Early in her career, McCormick often performed difficult dives usually attempted only by men and which were actually outlawed in international competition until 1952. McCormick's Olympic training regimen included a two-and-one half hour drill on the 33-foot high platform, then two hours of springboard practice daily, plus an evening three-hour workout, totaling 80 to 100 dives per day, six days a week. It was her way of fine-tuning her skills by demanding more from herself than she would actually need.

Following her Olympic performance in 1956, McCormick won the James E. Sullivan Award that year as the outstanding amateur athlete in the United States. After her triumphs in the 1956 Olympics, McCormick retired from competition and operated a diving camp for a number of years.

In 1984, McCormick was a member of the escort group for the U.S. flag at the opening ceremonies of that year's Olympics. At those Games, her daughter Kelly won a silver medal in the springboard event.

Considered by many baseball experts to be the greatest all-around player in history, **Willie Mays** could do it all on the diamond: hit with power, run like a deer, field as if he had invented the center field position, and throw with a cannon-like arm.

In his hometown of Westfield, Alabama, Mays was such a complete baseball player even at a young age that he was playing with adults on his father's steel mill team when he was just 14 years old. When he was old enough to turn professional, the major league's color line was still in effect, so Mays wound up signing with the Birmingham Black Barons of the Negro Leagues in 1947.

However, fortunately for Mays and other black players, the world was changing. That same year, **Jackie Robinson** shattered the color barrier, and the previously all-white National and American ball clubs began raiding the Negro League teams to sign their best players. A player of Mays's caliber was certain to go quickly, and so he joined the New York Giants organization in 1950.

The Giants sent him down to their farm system where Mays quickly proved that he was ready for the big leagues. He was hitting .477 for the Minneapolis Millers in 1951 when he was called up to the parent club.

Initially Mays struggled with the Giants. However, Manager **Leo Durocher** saw something in the youngster and stuck with him. Mays rebounded to finish the 1951 season with a .274 average and 20 homers, totals that were good enough to win the Rookie of the Year Award. He helped lead the Giants' amazing comeback from 13 1/2 games back to overtake the Brooklyn Dodgers for the pennant.

Following two seasons lost to military service, Mays celebrated his return in 1954 by hitting .345 with 41 home runs and win-

ning the Most Valuable Player Award. He led the Giants to another pennant that year, along with a World Series title.

For the next decade and a half, the **Say Hey Kid** really tore up the National League. He led the league in homers four times, in steals four years in a row, knocked in more than 100 runs nine times, and consistently hit over .300.

In the field, Mays was simply spectacular. His hat had a habit of flying off whenever he made a difficult catch, and his trademark "basket catch" was the place where countless doubles and triples went to die.

By the time he retired, Mays had won two Most Valuable Player Awards and twelve Gold Gloves. He finished with a .302 lifetime batting average, 3,283 hits, 660 home runs, and 1,903 RBI.

Willie Mays

Willie Shoemaker is simply **"Mr. Horse Racing."** When he retired in 1990, he had 8,833 career victories—the most in the history of the sport.

Ironically, the greatest jockey in the history of racing wasn't expected to survive his own birth. A premature baby born on a cotton farm near Fabens, Texas, he weighed just two and one-half pounds when he came into the world, and the doctors were skeptical of his survival. However, his grandmother nurtured him in a shoe box she placed on the door of a warm oven, and Shoemaker overcame the dire predictions to grow up healthy.

Willie Shoemaker

He weighed 85 pounds in high school, and had tremendous strength for someone his size. He once won a boxing competition against boys of 100 pounds and over.

Reasoning that the best place for boys his size was the racetrack, Shoemaker worked as a groom and exercise boy at a ranch. He saved enough money to go to California and catch on as an exercise rider. When a trainer saw him working with and riding the animals, he was impressed enough to get him his first race.

Shoemaker didn't win his first race, but he did win his third. In fact, in his first year Shoemaker won 219 times. The next year, he won 388 times. In his third year he set an all-time record with 485 wins.

Thereafter, there was no stopping the four-foot eleven, 103-pound Shoemaker. He won the Belmont Stakes five times (1957, 1959, 1962, 1967, and 1975), the Kentucky Derby four times (1955, 1959, 1965, and 1986), and the Preakness twice (1963 and 1967). He was the leading money-winner among jockeys for seven consecutive years (1958-1964). In 1986, he became the oldest jockey to ever win the Kentucky Derby.

Between 1949 and 1990, Shoemaker rode in more than 40,250 races—more than any other jockey in history. He won more than $123 million in purses, another all-time record.

Shoemaker's racing style was as unique as the man himself. Prior to a race, he studied each horse's history, its wins and losses, trying to discern the motivations behind peak performance. He used the whip sparingly, and often hung back at the beginning of a race. He waited until his opponents had made their moves before he passed them. These techniques often helped him get surprising results out of underrated horses.

In 1990, Shoemaker retired from racing to become a horse trainer. In 1991, he suffered a devastating automobile accident that left him paralyzed, but showing his indomitable spirit, he continued to work with his beloved horses.

48. Johnny Unitas
(1933-2002) Football

The career of **Johnny Unitas** should be required reading for every struggling football player. Overlooked, underestimated, and then cut from his first pro team, he persevered and went on to become perhaps the greatest quarterback in National Football League history.

Unitas was born in Pittsburgh, Pennsylvania and went to college at the University of Louisville; he played quarterback there, but was virtually unknown nationally. Unitas's dream was to play pro football for his hometown Pittsburgh Steelers, and he initially got that chance after he was the Steelers' ninth-round draft choice in 1955. However, even though they were a sad-sack NFL team at this time, they were unimpressed with Unitas. He got virtually no playing time in training camp as a rookie, and the team cut him before the next season began.

Discouraged but not defeated, Unitas hooked up the following year with the NFL's Baltimore Colts. Before long, he was the team's starting quarterback.

At this time the NFL did not have the wide television exposure it has today; there was no Monday Night Football, and even Sunday telecasts were sparse, with the 12 NFL teams televising their games only on a regional basis. However, in 1958, Unitas quarterbacked the Colts to a thrilling, 23-17 overtime victory over the New York Giants in the NFL Championship game, a contest televised to a national TV audience. Called by many the greatest pro football game ever played, it did a lot to establish the NFL as an institution in the homes of sports fans everywhere.

Unitas again led the Colts to a victory over the Giants in the 1959 championship game. He was voted the MVP in both games. For much of the next decade, Unitas was in

his prime. He was voted Player of the Year three times, (1959, 1964, and 1967), led the league in TD passes four straight years (1957-1960), and in passing yardage four times. He also had three seasons when he threw for 3,000 yards or more, and was a ten-time Pro Bowl selection.

Johnny Unitas

During Unitas's era, the quarterbacks called their own plays, rather than the coaches, and Unitas was considered the most brilliant playcaller of his time. The great coach **Vince Lombardi** said of him, "He is uncanny in his abilities, under the most violent pressure, to pick out the soft spot in a defense."

When he retired after the 1974 season, Unitas had a total of 40,239 career passing yards and 290 touchdown passes. He was elected to the pro football Hall of Fame in 1979, and he was named the quarterback of the NFL's All-Time Team in 2000 by Hall of Fame voters.

49. Henry Aaron
(1934-) Baseball

As baseball's all-time home run champion, **Hank Aaron** will forever be known as the man who broke **Babe Ruth's** career record. However, he should also be remembered as the steadiest and most consistent hitter of his era, and one of the greatest all-around players in the history of the game.

The area of Mobile, Alabama, where Aaron was born and raised had a high school with no baseball team. Aaron practiced his baseball skills by hitting bottle caps with a broomstick and playing in sandlot games.

Aaron began his pro career in 1951 when he signed with the Indianapolis Clowns of the Negro Leagues. However, it was four years after **Jackie Robinson** (see no. 35) had broken major league baseball's color barrier, and black baseball as a separate entity was virtually finished. So, Aaron signed with the Boston Braves of the National League the following year, and spent the next two years in the minors.

In spring training 1954, the starting left fielder of the now-Milwaukee Braves broke his ankle. The team put Aaron in his place, and from that day forward, Aaron was a regular. In his first year, the rookie slammed 13 homers, and followed that with 27 homers and a .314 batting average his second year.

In 1956, Aaron won the NL batting title, with a .328 average, to go along with 26 homers. With Aaron as one of the main offensive catalysts, the Braves streaked to the National League pennant the next two years; in 1957 they beat the New York Yankees in the World Series, in large part because Aaron hit .393, with 3 home runs and 7 RBI.

Over the next 18 years, Aaron proceeded to turn in one of the most remarkable careers in baseball history. A model of consistency, he hit 30 or more homers 15 times, drove in more than 100 runs 11 times, and hit .300 or better 14 times. He led the league in home runs and RBI four times, won the batting title twice, and was the league's MVP in 1957.

At a time when many players begin to slow down, Aaron remarkably showed little effects from aging; he smashed 245 homers after he turned 35—a major league record.

On April 8th, 1974, this quiet, unassuming player belted his 715th home run, breaking Babe Ruth's record. As usual, he was the calm in the eye of the public storm that surrounded his quest for the record.

Upon retirement, Aaron had a record 755 home runs, along with a .305 batting average, and 2,297 RBI—another record. In 1982, he was elected to the baseball Hall of Fame.

Henry Aaron

50. Larissa Latynina
(1934-) Gymnastics

Larissa Latynina was the first female athlete to win nine gold medals at the Olympics, and her amazing success helped popularize gymnastics all over the world.

She was born in 1934 in Kherson, in the present-day republic of Ukraine, which at the time was part of the Soviet Union. As a child, Latynina trained as a ballet dancer, where her exceptional balance and poise were readily apparent. She went on to formal education at the Kiev State Institute of Physical Culture, and was a national schools gymnastic champion at the age of 16.

Latynina burst upon the international stage at the 1956 Olympics. There she won the individual All-Around Olympic Championship with a score of 74.933, and tied for first in the floor exercise, with 18.733 points.

She also won the vault event, and helped lead the Soviet team to victory in the combined competition.

Latynina routed the opposition at the 1957 and 1958 European championships, winning five individual events. In 1958 as well, she was the world champion on the uneven bars, the balance beam, and the vault.

Latynina then shone again at the 1960 Olympics, winning the floor exercise outright with a score of 19.583, and again taking the all-around championship with a score of 77.031. Again she helped lead the Soviets to victory in the overall team competition.

Two years later she once more won an all-around championship and was the world champion in the floor exercise. At the 1964 Olympics, she was victorious again in the floor exercise with a total of 19.599 points, while leading the Soviet team to another all-around victory.

In competing in three Olympics, in addition to her record nine gold medals, Latynina also won five silver and four bronze medals; her total of 18 Olympic medals made her the all-time overall leading medal winner. Latynina's astonishing career helped put kids on the parallel bars and the rings all over the world. In her homeland, she established a path that future gymnastics stars such as **Olga Korbut** would follow.

After she retired from competition, Latynina became a coach for the Soviet gymnastic team, and helped plan the 1980 Moscow Olympics.

Larissa Latynina

51. Bill Russell
(1934-) Basketball

He teamed with **Bob Cousy** to turn the Boston Celtics into a perennial NBA champion, and his battles with **Wilt Chamberlain** were legendary. He was defensive genius **Bill Russell**, one of the most dominant big men in the history of basketball.

Russell was born in Monroe, Louisiana in 1934, and suffered a great deal of racial discrimination as a child; that experience just made him that much more assertive about African-American rights as an adult. His family moved to Oakland, California, where Russell made his high school basketball team as a junior; at six foot, two inches, he was somewhat awkward, and was only a third string player.

Bill Russell

However, it was as a college player that Russell garnered national attention. He attended the University of San Francisco where, as a six foot, nine inch sophomore he became the team's starting center. Along with **K.C. Jones**, Russell turned the school into a basketball powerhouse. The team won 55 consecutive games at one point and won back-to-back NCAA titles in 1955 and 1956.

After helping the U.S. team win the gold medal in the 1956 Olympics, Russell was drafted by the NBA's Boston Celtics. There, along with playmaking genius Bob Cousy, he turned the team into a basketball juggernaut.

Russell added the necessary defensive ingredients—mainly shot-blocking and rebounding—to Cousy's play-making wizardry to turn the Celtics into an unstoppable force. Boston won the NBA championship in Russell's first year, finished second the following season, then reeled off a run of eight straight titles beginning in 1959.

Russell was voted the NBA's Most Valuable Player four times (1958, 1961, 1962, and 1963). He had 21,620 career rebounds, averaged more than 22 rebounds per game, and led the league in rebounding four times. He also scored more than 14,000 points in his career.

Russell and the great Wilt Chamberlain (see no. 54) were the two most dominating players in the league during the 1960s, and their battles on the hard court were classic. While Chamberlain was an unstoppable offensive force, Russell was a better rebounder and shot blocker, and aided by a much better supporting cast, the Celtics usually came out on top in their head-to-head battles.

In 1966, Russell became the first African-American coach in major professional sports when he was named the player-coach of the Celtics. He then led them to back-to-back championships in 1968 and 1969. In Russell's career, he won 11 NBA titles in 13 seasons, a record that will almost certainly never be surpassed.

Russell subsequently coached the NBA's Seattle Supersonics and Sacramento Kings, and he was elected to the basketball Hall of Fame in 1974.

52. A.J. Foyt
(1935-) Auto Racing

The first four-time winner of the Indianapolis 500, **Anthony Joseph "A.J." Foyt** is one of the all-time greats in the history of auto racing.

Foyt was born in Houston, Texas, with gasoline in his veins. His father was a garage owner and midget car racer who was a mechanical genius. He could wring every available foot-pound of horsepower from a gasoline engine.

The young Foyt won his first race at the age of five, in a car his dad built. Thoroughly bitten by the racing bug, he left high school to become a mechanic and begin his racing career. He was so good that he dominated the tracks where he lived. He moved on the Midwest at the age of 18, driving against the big names in auto racing during the 1950s. It didn't matter to Foyt what type of car he drove—sprints, midgets, stocks—as long as he could race them.

That type of burning competitive desire gave Foyt a reputation that he carried with him when he joined the United States Auto Club (USAC) in preparation for racing in the Indianapolis 500. His first USAC event was driving a midget racer in 1956.

In 1958, Foyt qualified for the 500. He drove in the prestigious race in one of the legendary Dean Van Lines Specials and finished 16th.

Three years later Foyt won his first Indy 500, a feat he would repeat in 1964, 1967, and 1977, setting new speed records with the first two victories.

In his career, Foyt won seven USAC championships—1960, 1961, 1963, 1964, 1967, 1975, and 1979. Among the major races he

A.J. Foyt

has won are the 1972 Daytona 500 and the 24 Hours of Le Mans in 1967. He also won the 24 Hours of Daytona twice, in 1983 and 1985.

Foyt had a unique career in auto racing in that he drove virtually every type of car, except for professional drag racers. He also continued to enjoy considerable success as he got older, although auto racing is typically a young man's sport.

Despite suffering injuries several times in crashes over the years, Foyt continued his legendary career until 1993. Fittingly, he announced his retirement during the qualifying trials for the Indianapolis 500.

59

53. Sandy Koufax
(1935-) Baseball

Sandy Koufax

Although the brilliant years of his career spanned only six seasons, there can be no doubt to anyone who ever saw him pitch that **Sandy Koufax** was one of the greatest pitchers in baseball history.

Born in Brooklyn, New York, Koufax was a star athlete in high school, but his sport was basketball, not baseball. In 1953, he attended the University of Cincinnati on a basketball scholarship. However, when he heard that the baseball team was going on a trip to New Orleans, he couldn't resist joining up to go along.

Although he initially played first base, his hitting was so poor that he moved to the mound. There he displayed a blazing fastball, but little control. However, his hometown Brooklyn Dodgers decided to take a chance on him and signed him for $20,000.

Under a rule in effect in baseball at the time, Koufax was forced to remain on the major league roster, rather than go to the minors for seasoning. So his first few years were a struggle, as he compiled middling won-lost records. Even when he had a big game, such as when he struck out a record-tying 18 batters, he would slip back into mediocrity.

Then, in a spring training game in 1961, his catcher told Koufax to slow down his delivery of his fastball, to get better control of the pitch. Koufax tried the new approach, and it worked—to perfection. After two strong years in 1961 and 1962, he turned in four consecutive brilliant seasons in which he simply dominated the league's hitters.

From 1963 through 1966, Koufax pitched 1,192 innings, struck out 1,228 batters, completed 60 percent of his starts, allowed only 6.2 hits per nine innings, and hurled 31 shutouts. His won-lost record was a sparkling 97-27, a .782 percentage. His yearly won-lost totals were 25-5, 19-5, 26-8 and 27-9.

During his career, Koufax pitched four no-hitters, including one perfect game. He led the league in wins three times, in earned run average five times, and in strikeouts four times. In 1963, he won both the National League's Cy Young and Most Valuable Player Awards. Along with **Don Drysdale**, Koufax provided the Dodgers with as potent a one-two pitching combination as there ever had been in baseball. The Dodgers won the World Series in 1963 and 1965, and Koufax threw the championship-clinching games in each Series.

At the conclusion of the 1966 season, an arthritic elbow forced Koufax to retire when he was still in his prime. He was elected to the baseball Hall of Fame in 1972.

54. Wilt Chamberlain
(1936-1999) Basketball

Wilt Chamberlain was an unstoppable force in basketball. Although he never achieved the type of championship success that **Bill Russell** (see no. 51) did, nevertheless Chamberlain is remembered as perhaps the most dominating offensive presence the game has ever seen.

He was born in Philadelphia, and even though his parents were both of average size, Chamberlain had already reached a height of six feet by the age of ten. In school he wanted to be a track and field star, and dreamed of competing in the Olympics as a sprinter. However, his height—he was nearly seven feet tall when he was in high school—literally compelled him to play basketball. He led his team, Philadelphia's Overbrook High School, to three public school championships and two all-city titles.

Not surprisingly, every college in the country vied for Chamberlain, and the University of Kansas was the winner. Over his two-year college career, he averaged 29.9 points and 18.3 rebounds per game. He was named College Player of the Year in 1957.

Chamberlain left college after his junior year to play with the Harlem Globetrotters for one season. In 1959, he was selected by the National Basketball Association's Philadelphia Warriors in the draft, and the 7-1 foot, 275 pound giant immediately turned that team into an NBA powerhouse. He averaged 37.6 points and 27 rebounds during his first season, earning both

Rookie of the Year and Most Valuable Player honors.

By his third season (1961-62), Chamberlain was reaching nearly unimaginable heights as a player. He averaged an astonishing 50.4 points that season with 25.7 rebounds. On March 2, 1962, he had perhaps the greatest individual game in NBA history by pouring in 100 points as the Warriors defeated the New York Knicks 169-147. Chamberlain scored 31 points in the final period alone.

However, despite his individual success, Chamberlain's couldn't lead his team to an NBA title, generating charges that he wasn't a team player and couldn't win the big games. His battles under the basket with Bill Russell of the Celtics were classic, but Russell, who benefited from a better supporting cast of players, almost always emerged victorious. Finally, in 1967, playing for a Philadelphia 76ers team with other talented players, Chamberlain earned his first championship.

Traded in 1968 to the Los Angeles Lakers, Chamberlain again shared the scoring spotlight with other great players, such as **Jerry West**; in 1972, the Lakers had one of the greatest seasons in history, and Chamberlain had another championship. He played one more season, then retired.

Chamberlain left the game with numerous records, including most points (31,419) and most rebounds (23,924). In 1978, he was elected to the basketball Hall of Fame.

Wilt Chamberlain

Jim Brown played professional football for only nine seasons, but during that time he managed to become perhaps the greatest running back in National Football League history.

Born in 1936 on St. Simon's Island, Georgia, he eventually moved to the New York City area when he was seven. An excellent high school athlete in several sports, he was considered one of the best school athletes in New York history.

Brown's fiercely independent streak showed itself when he chose to attend Syracuse University, one of the few colleges that had not offered him an athletic scholarship. (He was offered a total of 42 athletic scholarships.) A friend of his who wanted him to succeed pooled money from a group of Jim Brown fans and they paid his way to college.

Jim Brown

At Syracuse, Brown won ten varsity letters: two each in track and baseball, and three each in lacrosse and football. He was an All-American in lacrosse and football.

After he graduated from Syracuse, Brown turned down $150,000 to become a professional fighter. Instead, he joined the NFL after the Cleveland Browns drafted him for the 1957 season. Brown was the Rookie of the Year that season, when he gained 942 yards on 202 carries. In one game against the Los Angeles Rams, he set a rushing record of 237 yards, scoring four touchdowns as well.

Over the next eight seasons Brown was virtually unstoppable as he rampaged through the rest of the NFL. He scored a record 126 career touchdowns, led the league in rushing yardage seven times, was named to the All-Pro team eight times, and was the Most Valuable Player twice.

At 6 foot, 2 inches tall and 228 pounds, Brown combined excellent speed with elusive moves. While he rarely ran over an opponent, his quickness and power allowed him to break many off-balance tackles.

Brown rushed for over 1,000 yards in seven seasons, over 200 yards in a game four times, and over 100 yards in a game 54 times. Remarkably, he never missed a game because of an injury. Even more surprising, Brown established his rushing marks in seasons that contained 12, or at the most, 14, games. In 1963, Brown became the first football player to gain more than a mile in a season when he rushed for a total of 1,863 yards.

No one knows what other rushing records he could have set, but Brown retired at the conclusion of the 1966 season to pursue an acting career. He finished with 12,312 lifetime yards, the most in NFL history at the time. He was voted into the pro football Hall of Fame in 1971.

The first stock car driver to win $1 million in prize money, **Richard Petty** retired as the all-time leader in victories on the professional stock car circuit.

Born in North Carolina, Petty, like **A.J. Foyt** (see no. 52), grew up in the world of auto racing. His father was **Lee Petty**, an early National Association of Stock Car Auto Racing (NASCAR) champion. The younger Petty often said that he became a race car driver because his father was one, and he enjoyed the entire auto racing environment.

Petty began his career as a mechanic for his father, and he first got behind the wheel when he was 21 years old. In 1959, Petty raced in the first Daytona 500, but his car broke down after 20 miles; his father wound up winning the race. However, the young Petty did well enough in that race and others to be named the NASCAR Rookie of the Year. The following year, Petty won his first race. From that point on, he was a solid, consistent driver.

Then, in 1964, things changed for Petty. Plymouth, which had been Petty's informal sponsor, decided to fully back his efforts. Before that, Plymouth's casual approach to auto racing meant that the Petty cars were sometimes up against higher-horsepower competition. Now, with Plymouth's full commitment, Petty was able to utilize the new Chrysler 426 hemispherical combustion chamber engine with high-end torque. That engine helped Petty establish dominance over the stock car racing world.

The difference that the new engine made in Petty's racing could be seen in the Daytona 500 that year. Petty won the event by setting a new world speed record of 154.3 miles per hour. That year, 1964, was also the year that Petty won his first NASCAR national championship.

Now there was no stopping "King Richard" and his famous chalk-blue "Number 43" Plymouth. He became a major force in stock car racing, helping to push the sport to new heights of popularity. In 1966, he became the first driver to win two Daytona 500's, and the following year he set a record by winning 27 races. He won a third Daytona 500 in 1971, as well as the Dixie 500, and earned more than $1 million in prize money. In 1979, he became the first owner-driver to win the Winston Cup.

Richard Petty

Upon his retirement after the 1992 season, Petty had won the Daytona 500 7 times, was the NASCAR national driving champion 7 times, and was the all-time NASCAR leader in wins with 200. When he retired, Petty formed Petty Enterprises, a complete stock-car racing enterprise.

57. Rod Laver
(1938-) Tennis

Rod Laver is the only player to twice win the grand slam of tennis—Wimbledon, and the Australian, French, and U.S. Open championships in a single year.

He was born in Rockhampton, Queensland, Australia in 1938; a sickly child, he seemed an unlikely candidate for future tennis stardom. However, even though he was small for a tennis player, he developed a devastating topspin ground stroke that befuddled opponents. He was the Australian junior champion in 1957.

From 1959 to 1962, Laver was a member of the Australian Davis Cup team, which went undefeated during those years. In 1960, Laver won the men's singles title at the Australian championship, and followed that up in 1961 by winning the men's singles title at Wimbledon.

Rod Laver

The next year, Laver won his first grand slam. He also won the Italian, Netherlands, Norwegian, and Swiss championships in 1962—an unprecedented feat demonstrating his total domination over the sport. It was little wonder that he was proclaimed the world's greatest tennis player that year.

Laver used a variety of shots to become a great tennis player. He had a powerful volley stroke and a unique, spinning serve that was difficult to effectively return. His forehand and backhand were widely considered the best in tennis history.

Laver turned pro in 1963, and suffered a devastating beginning to his professional career—he lost 14 of his first 16 matches. However, he maintained his game, and by 1965, he had turned things around completely.

As an amateur, Laver was rated Number One in 1961 and 1962, and then, when he became professional he was considered the world's top player from 1965 to 1967. (Pros weren't officially rated until 1968.) Subsequently, he was officially ranked Number One as a pro in 1968 and 1969.

In 1968, Laver won Wimbledon for the third time and was the first professional to win the tournament. Then he had perhaps his greatest year ever in 1969 when he won 17 singles titles, including his second grand slam. Winning a second grand slam was an unprecedented feat in tennis history.

Throughout his illustrious career, Laver won eight grand slam doubles championships and had 47 tournament victories. He won four Wimbledons, three Australian, two French and two U.S. championships. Showing how completely dominant he was in the tennis world, Laver was rated a Top Ten player until 1975, at age 37, in what traditionally has been a young person's sport.

Jack Nicklaus has been called the greatest golfer of all time, and why not? No one who has ever picked up a golf club can compare with the **Golden Bear** in his prime, who the Professional Golf Association (PGA) honored as the Golfer of the Century in 1988.

Born in Columbus Ohio, in 1940, Nicklaus inherited a love of sports from his athletic father. The young Nicklaus excelled in football, basketball, baseball, and track as well as golf, which he began playing at age 10. Six years later he won his first tournament—the Ohio Open—and knew that golf was indeed his game.

Nicklaus concentrated on golf during his college years at Ohio State University in the late 1950s and early 1960s. In 1959, while playing on the U.S. Walker Cup team, he won two of his matches, and played a significant role in the American team's victory. Unsure of his ability before that, he now understood his true potential.

In 1959 and again in 1961, Nicklaus won the U.S. Amateur championship. However, it was in 1960 that Nicklaus began writing his own legend. That year he came in second to the great **Arnold Palmer** in the U.S. Open. Nicklaus's 282 over 72 holes was the best score ever by an amateur to that date. Between 1959 and 1961, he won all but one of the amateur tournaments he entered.

In November 1961, Nicklaus turned pro, and while he didn't win any of the 17 tournaments he entered, he always finished in the money.

In 1962, he defeated Palmer in a playoff for the U.S. Open title, becoming the youngest player ever to win the tournament, and beginning a heated rivalry between the two men.

Over the years Nicklaus won six Masters Tournaments, five PGA championships, three more U.S. Opens, three British Open titles,

Jack Nicklaus

six Australian Opens, and one World Open. A five-time PGA Player of the Year, his final Masters victory in 1986, at the age of 46, made him the oldest champion in its history. He was also a six-time Ryder Cup team member.

After he joined the senior tour in 1990, Nicklaus won the Senior Open tournament in 1991 and 1993. He has also won numerous sportsman of the year awards, and was *Sports Illustrated's* Athlete of the Decade in 1980.

During the course of his career Nicklaus has designed many golf courses, and in 1993 *Golf World* Magazine named him Architect of the Year. Some of the courses he has designed routinely make lists of the top 100 golf courses in America.

59. Mario Andretti
(1940-) Auto Racing

As the winner of the Daytona 500, the Indianapolis 500, and the Formula One World Championship, **Mario Andretti** is one of the most successful and versatile race car drivers in history.

Born in Montona, an Italian village on the Adriatic Sea, Andretti learned about auto racing and race cars at an early age. He went to see the *Mille Miglia* (Thousand Miles) race as a boy, and was completely hooked. With a motorcycle and a small coupe, he and his brother Aldo began racing.

Mario Andretti

The brothers didn't miss a beat when the Andretti family moved halfway across the globe to Nazareth, Pennsylvania in 1955. They worked as mechanics and bought a modified 1948 Hudson to run on the stock car ovals. Initially Aldo was the ace driver, but an accident at the track in Hatfield, Pennsylvania forced him to the sidelines. Mario moved behind the wheel, running modifieds, midgets, and three-quarter midgets, working as a mechanic by day and a driver by night. On Labor Day, 1963, he won three races at Hatfield and four at Flemington, New Jersey. Those seven same-day victories convinced him that he was ready for the big time.

Even though his first United States Auto Club (USAC) race in 1964 resulted in a spin-out, his racing was impressive enough that he was offered a car to race by another racing team. It didn't take long for Andretti to prove that he truly belonged behind the wheel. In 1965, he became the USAC points champion and also had the fastest time for the first qualifying heats of the Indianapolis 500; overall he finished third in the race.

The following year Andretti was again the UASC points champion. He also set a record by leading for 500 consecutive miles of championship racing, winning the Atlanta 300, Milwaukee 100, and the Langhorne 100. He began driving Championship GT cars, running a Ferrari to victory at Sebring. He also set a new lap record at Le Mans of 3:23.6.

In 1967, Andretti won the Daytona 500 in a Holman & Moody-prepared Ford Fairlaine. Two years later, he won the Indianapolis 500.

During the 1970s, it was Grand Prix Formula One racing that commanded the bulk of Andretti's attention. He won the Formula One championship in 1978. He then returned to Indy car racing.

Before he retired in 1994, Andretti had recorded four USAC/CART Championships, the 1965 Indy Rookie of the Year award, and second place on the all-time win list for Indy cars, with 51 victories. He also had the satisfaction of seeing his sons Michael and Jeff become excellent race car drivers as well.

60. Pelé
(1940-) Soccer

One of the most recognizable athletes in the entire world, **Pelé** helped create a soccer boom in the United States with his athletic skills and charisma.

Pelé was born **Edson Arantes do Nascimento** in Tres Coracoes, Brazil. His father was a soccer pro, but bad knees forced him to retire. His son inherited his love of the game, and Pelé and the neighborhood children played soccer from dawn to dusk, using a sock stuffed with newspapers and wadded up as a ball. His father coached him, and Pelé and his friends played other local teams.

Soon Pelé was playing on the junior squad of the Bauru city team. He led them to the junior championship three years in a row. He then signed with Santos, a professional team, and scored a league record 17 goals in his first year.

Chosen for the Brazilian World Cup team in 1958, he helped lead his country to the championship when they defeated Sweden 5-2. Pelé also led Brazil to the world title in 1962 and 1970, becoming the only player to be a member of three World Cup title teams.

Pelé's role in bringing championships to his team cannot be over- estimated. Known for his powerful kicks and uncanny ball control, he was able to pass the ball to teammates at will, often without looking. Another facet of Pelé's game was his brilliant field strategy.

Pelé was an international hero whose presence once stopped a war between Biafra and Nigeria because both sides wanted to see him play. Pope **Paul VI** once said to him, "Don't be nervous, my son. I am more nervous than you, for I have been waiting to meet Pelé personally for a long time."

In 1970, Pelé scored his 1,000th goal, making him the most prolific goal scorer in history. He retired from Brazilian team World Cup play in 1970, and then from Santos team club play in 1974. However, **Clive Toye**, president of the New York City Cosmos of the North American Soccer League, begged him to play in America and "go down in history as the man who truly brought soccer to the United States."

Pelé

Pelé played for the Cosmos from 1975 to 1977, leading them to a league championship in 1977. His contract with the Cosmos made him the highest paid athlete in the world, and he brought his mystique and an unbelievable level of excitement to the games, helping to popularize soccer in America.

After his final retirement in 1977, Pelé became an international goodwill ambassador for the sport.

67

61. Vasili Alexeyev
(1942-) Weightlifting

Two-time Olympic gold medal winner, and eight time world champion, **Vasili Alexeyev** was one of the greatest weightlifters in the history of the sport.

He was born in Pokrov in the Soviet Union in 1942. He worked in a timber/logging camp as a youth, and impressed many with the ease with which he moved massive logs. It is said that his first barbell was the wheels and axle of a timber camp truck. Once for breakfast he was reported to have eaten 26 fried eggs and a steak.

Alexeyev first burst upon the world weightlifting scene on June 24, 1970. That day, he set three world records: the clean and jerk (488.3 pounds), the press (464.1 pounds), and the three-lift total (1,311.7 pounds). Then in September of that year, he jerked a weight in excess of 500 pounds, breaking a weightlifting barrier as significant as the four-minute mile in track.

Two years later, at the 1972 Olympics, Alexeyev won the gold medal in the super heavyweight class. He set world records in all four categories of the weightlifting competition: the clean and jerk (507.1 pounds), the press (518.1 pounds), the snatch (385.8 pounds) and the three-lift total (1,411 pounds).

Four years later, at the 1976 Olympics, Alexeyev was again the story in the weightlifting competition. He broke his own record in the clean and jerk with a lift of 562.2 pounds; his two-lift total—the press had been eliminated from the competition—of 970 pounds gave him another gold medal.

Incredibly, Alexeyev stayed undefeated in the super heavyweight competition from 1970 through 1978, setting 80 world records from 1970-1977.

Unfortunately, Alexeyev was injured at the 1978 world championships and his brilliant career went into decline. Nevertheless, before his retirement, Alexeyev accomplished weightlifitng feats no other athlete had ever attained before.

Vasili Alexeyev

He said he could "float like a butterfly and sting like a bee," and as the only three-time heavyweight champion, there was little doubt that **Muhammad Ali** could do all that—and a whole lot more.

Born **Cassius Marcellus Clay, Jr.** in Louisville, Kentucky in 1942, he took up boxing as a youth. By the time he was 18, Clay had fought in more than 100 amateur fights and compiled a record of 108 wins and 8 losses. In 1960, he took home a gold medal as the light heavyweight champion at the Olympics.

When he returned from the Olympics, Clay turned professional. With the reputable **Angelo Dundee** as his trainer, Clay won his first pro fight on October 29, 1960. By the autumn of 1962 he had won 16 straight bouts. He had a penchant of making up poetry, and predicting the round in which an opponent would fall, so he was dubbed the **Louisville Lip** by the sporting press.

In 1964, he fought and defeated **Sonny Liston** for the heavyweight championship of the world in a huge upset. The following year he defeated Liston in a rematch; in between the two bouts, Clay became a Muslim and took the name Muhammad Ali.

Ali successfully defended his title several times. Then, in 1967, he refused induction into the U.S. military on the grounds that he was a conscientious objector. He was stripped of his title and banned from boxing.

After a nearly four year absence, Ali returned to boxing in 1970 when a court ordered New York to restore his license. The next year, the U.S. Supreme Court overturned his conviction on appeal. In March of 1971, he fought **Joe Frazier**, who had become the champ in the interim, inaugurating a series of fights with Frazier that would become legendary. Ali lost that bout, but he beat Frazier in January, 1974, earning the right to battle

George Foreman for the heavyweight title that he had subsequently taken from Frazier.

Muhammad Ali

The fight with Foreman was held in Zaire, and dubbed, "The Rumble in the Jungle." Although Foreman was younger, Ali was more resourceful, and upset the champion. Ali then fought Frazier and beat him again, in a classic slugfest known as, "The Thrilla in Manila."

After successfully defending the title several more times, Ali lost it in February, 1978, to **Leon Spinks**. Ali then fought Spinks again, this time regaining the heavyweight title for the third time. After retiring in 1979, Ali tried an abortive comeback, but lost two more fights and retired for good.

Ali retired with a record of 56-5, and a legacy as one of the greatest, and one of the most controversial, heavyweight champions of all time.

The winner of 24 grand slam singles championships, more than any other woman, **Margaret Smith Court** is one of the greatest players in the history of women's tennis.

She was born Margaret Jean Smith in Albury, New South Wales, Australia. Upon winning the 1960 Australian championships—later the Australian Open— Smith became known for her rocket-like serve and volley. She went on to win that tournament ten more times, including a run of seven consecutive titles from 1960-1966.

In 1962, she won her first international tournament—the U.S. Singles championship (the present-day U.S. Open). The following year she became the first Australian woman to win at Wimbledon, which she won again in 1965. In 1966, Smith married **Barry Court**, had a child, and intended to retire. However, there was a lot of tennis left in her future.

Encouraged by her husband, who became her manager, she stepped back out onto the court. Now known as Margaret Smith Court, she won the Australian, French, and U.S. Open titles in 1969. Then in 1970, she swept all four major titles—the Australian, French, and U.S. Opens, plus Wimbledon—at the time becoming only the second woman to win the grand slam in singles play. Her 46-game victory over **Billie Jean King** at Wimbledon was the longest women's single final in that tournament's history.

Smith Court had another child in 1972, but returned once more to competition the following year. She traveled with her husband, two children, and a nanny, and had another outstanding year, winning three of the four grand slam events—the Australian, French, and U.S. Opens. She also lost a highly-publicized match with 55-year-old **Bobby Riggs**, who was defeated later that year by Billie Jean King.

By 1973, she had won 61 major championships. That year, she was also the leading money winner on the Virginia Slims circuit with winnings of $180,058.

During her career, she won 24 singles titles, 19 women's doubles titles, and 19 mixed doubles titles in grand slam tournaments; she also became the only player to win a grand slam in doubles and singles play. Her total of 62 grand slam titles is the most by any woman.

A national hero in her native country, she was elected to the International Tennis Hall of Fame in 1979.

Margaret Smith Court

64. Larry Mahan
(1943-) Rodeo

Rodeo cowboy is not a profession commonly thought of as producing great athletes, but in **Larry Mahan**, it might have produced the greatest rider of them all.

He was born on November 21, 1943 in Brooks, Oregon, and began riding in the rodeo at a children's competition in 1956. By 1962, Mahan had become the All-Around Oregon Cowboy champion, as well as emerging triumphant in the bareback bronc riding and bulldogging events.

In 1963, Mahan joined the Rodeo Cowboys Association, and began winning often in his signature events of bareback bronc and saddle bronc riding. In the bull riding category, he won so often that he was the top money winner in the event in 1965.

In 1966, Mahan was the first cowboy to compete in three Rodeo Nationals final events. That year was also the beginning of his record, five-year consecutive streak of winning the All-Around Cowboy title.

Mahan earned so much in winnings that he was able to buy his own private plane with which to travel to competitive events on the busy rodeo circuit. In 1967, he became the first rodeo star to earn more than $50,000 in a year. By 1971, he had earned in excess of $280,000 over his career—another record. He became a media star as well, appearing on television and helping to popularize the rodeo cowboy lifestyle.

Mahan credited his successful career in rodeo to his love of horses. Horses are "my passion," he says. "Dad always had horses around. And it was horses that brought me into the rodeo."

Larry Mahan

In the early 1970s, Mahan suffered an injury, and after winning his sixth All-Around Cowboy title in 1973, he retired.

In his subsequent years, Mahan spent time at his rodeo schools for youngsters, and tending to various business interests. He also wrote a book, *Fundamentals of Rodeo Riding, a Mental and Physical Approach to Success*, and starred in a 1973 movie, *The Great American Cowboy*.

One of soccer's great innovators, **Franz Beckenbauer** originated an offensive use for the sweeper position, which revolutionized the tactics of the sport.

Beckenbauer was born on September 11,1945 in Munich, in what would soon become postwar West Germany. Even as a youth, he showed a keen grasp of both the offensive and defensive sides of soccer, and would lead to his being recognized as a brilliant tactician and field general of the sport.

Beckenbauer joined the Bayern youth soccer team at the age of 14; three years later, he gave up his job as a trainee insurance salesman to become a professional soccer player.

Franz Beckenbauer

After struggling for a number of years, Beckenbauer's Bayern Munich club won the West German Cup in both 1966 and 1967. In 1971, Beckenbauer was made team captain, and beginning in 1974, he led them to three straight European titles. It was also in 1974 that he captained the West German team to a thrilling 2-1 World Cup victory over Holland in the championship game in his home city of Munich.

Beckenbauer won the European Player of the Year Award twice, in 1972 and 1976. However, perhaps his most lasting contribution to the sport of soccer was to make a mid-career switch from midfielder to sweeper, and then turn that position into an offensive one. Traditionally, the sweeper had been purely a defensive position, but Beckenbauer's slashing style and aggressive play changed the sweeper into an offensive catalyst.

This radically changed the sport, creating a style of "total soccer," which meant that all players had to be ready to function wherever they were on the field.

In 1977, Beckenbauer took his aggressive play across the ocean to America when he joined the New York Cosmos of the North American Soccer League (NASL). Since he joined a team that already had **Pelé** (see no. 60), this meant that the Cosmos had the two best soccer players in the entire world.

Beckenbauer was voted the NASL Player of the Year in 1977. He helped lead the Cosmos to NASL championships in 1977, 1978, and 1980.

After retiring as a player, Beckenbauer became the manager of the West German World Cup team in 1984. In 1990, he coached the team to a championship over Argentina, becoming the only person ever to have won the World Cup as both a player and a manager.

66. Sawao Kato
(1946-) Gymnastics

One of the great gymnasts in modern history, **Sawao Kato** demonstrated his complete dominance over the sport by winning gold medals in three different Olympics.

Born in 1946 in Japan, Kato worked hard and often as a youth in his quest to win Olympic gold. In this effort he was part of a nation-wide movement that made Japan a major force in Olympic gymnastic competition beginning in 1960 up to the present day.

By the time of the 1968 Mexico City Olympics, Kato was ready to demonstrate his ability to the world. At those Olympics, he was the gold medalist in the individual all-around and floor exercise events, and the bronze medalist in the rings. In addition, he was part of the Japanese team that won the gold in the all-around team competition.

Four years later, Kato again led the Japanese team to victory in the all- around team exercises at the 1972 Munich Olympics. Individually, he was the gold medalist in the all-around and parallel bars, and also won silver medals in the pommel horse and the horizontal bars events.

In the 1976 Montreal Olympics, Kato was again the star. He was the gold medalist in the parallel bars, and also took home a silver medal in the all-around category. In addition, he helped lead Japan to its third straight gold medal in the all-around team competition.

That made a total of eight gold medals that Kato had won in the three Olympics—more than any other male gymnast. He also won three silver medals and one bronze, ranking him high on the all-time list of Olympic medal winners. In 2001, Sawao Kato was inducted into the International Gymnastics Hall of Fame.

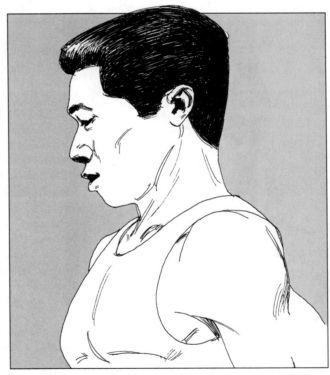

Sawao Kato

Laffit Pincay, Jr. won the most races of anybody in horse racing history.

A native of Panama City, Panama, Pincay had horse racing in his genes—his father was also a jockey. When he was 15, Pincay made his first move toward following in his father's footsteps by getting a job at a track as a hot-walker and mucking out stalls. He worked for several hours a day, then went to school from mid-afternoon to early evening. The young boy impressed people around the track with his horse-handling skills, and soon he was riding horses out of the gate.

Laffit Pincay, Jr.

Pincay won his first race in 1964, on only his second career ride. Shortly thereafter he came to the United States, where he won eight of his first eleven races. However, he spoke only Spanish and had to teach himself English by watching "Hollywood Squares" on television.

Pincay battled a lifelong weight problem, and that probably contributed to a collapse he suffered in the jockey's room in 1974 at Aqueduct Racetrack in New York. He re-examined his life, changed his diet, and emerged from his health ordeal leaner, stronger, and healthier.

Pincay was named the winner of the Eclipse Award for outstanding jockey of the year five times—1971, 1973, 1974, 1979, and 1985. It was the most number of times anybody has ever won that prestigious honor.

Pincay won the Belmont Stakes, one of horse racing's premier events, three years in a row (1982-84). In 1984, he also won the Kentucky Derby. In 1985 he became the first jockey in history to earn over $13 million in a single year.

Pincay has won six Breeders' Cup races, which are run to determine thoroughbred racing's principal champions in different classes. However, the pinnacle of his career came in 1999, when he won his 8,834th race, eclipsing the legendary **Willie Shoemaker's** record victory total. The win also pushed his lifetime earnings to more than $270 million—another record.

Four years later, Pincay was still going strong. In January 2003, at the age of 56, he reached another career milestone, winning his 9,500th and 9,501st races at Santa Anita Park in California. However, in March, he was severely injured when another horse swung wide, knocked him off his mount, and rolled on him.

Pincay broke two bones in his neck, and while the breaks healed, his doctors advised him that his spine was not sufficiently stable to allow him to ride again. In April, Pincay announced he would retire from racing. His final victory total was 9,530.

Lafitt Pincay, Jr. was elected to horse racing's Hall of Fame in 1975.

Kareem Abdul-Jabbar, pro basketball's all-time leading scorer, greatly changed the dynamics of the game's center position.

He was born **Ferdinand Lewis Alcindor,** in New York City in 1947, and first played basketball as a fourth-grade student. He was six feet, ten inches tall—and still growing—by the time he attended Powell Memorial high school. Like **Wilt Chamberlain** had done in high school, Alcindor dominated the sport. In his first year, Alcindor led the team to 27 victories and the Catholic

Kareem Abdul-Jabbar

League championship. By the end of his senior year, Powell Memorial had won 71 games in a row and had won three straight league titles. During his high school career, Alcindor set a New York City record for total points (2,067) and rebounds (2,002).

Attending college at the University of California at Los Angeles, he led the school's basketball team to three straight National Collegiate Athletic Association (NCAA) championships. He was named Most Valuable Player of the NCAA tournament three times, and was named College Player of the Year twice. It was also while he was at UCLA that he became a member of the Muslim faith, and then changed his name to Kareem Abdul-Jabbar.

The 7 foot, 1 inch center turned professional in 1969, joining the Milwaukee Bucks of the National Basketball Association. In 1971, he led them to the NBA championship.

In 1975, Abdul-Jabbar was traded to the Los Angeles Lakers. He immediately turned that team into perennial NBA championship contenders. During the 1980s, along with such stars as **Magic Johnson** and **James Worthy**, Abdul-Jabbar led the Lakers to five championship titles.

Although he was very tall, Abdul-Jabbar was not a big and bulky man. Rather, he was almost skinny for a NBA center. However, he brought a grace and fluidity to the position that had not been seen there before. With his unique "sky hook" shot that was nearly unstoppable, Abdul-Jabbar demonstrated that an NBA big man could do more than just intimidate opponents and grab rebounds. He could move around the court, get out of the paint to help his teammates on defense, and score from many different places.

Abdul-Jabbar was named the NBA's Most Valuable Player six times during the regular season (1971, 1972, 1974, 1976, 1977 and 1980) and twice during the playoffs (1971 and 1985).

When he retired in 1989 after a stellar 20-year career, Abdul-Jabbar was the all-time NBA leader in points scored, with 38,387. He was also the leader in 19 other categories, including blocked shots, field goal attempts, and field goal completions. He was voted into the basketball Hall of Fame in 1994.

69. Dan Gable
(1948-) Wrestling

Winner of a gold medal in the 1972 Olympics, **Dan Gable** was both a highly successful wrestler and a coach of the sport.

Born in Waterloo, Iowa, Gable did not lose a varsity wrestling match in high school. He continued this remarkable streak in college at Iowa State University until the final match of his senior year. Overall, his record in high school and college was 182-1.

Gable was a two-time National Collegiate Athletic Association (NCAA) champion, in 1969 and 1970. In 1969, he was voted the NCAA tournament's Most Outstanding Wrestler.

For the next three years, Gable dedicated himself to one goal—training for the Olympics. He trained seven hours a day, every day, in preparation for the 1972 Games. Prior to that, Gable entered other competitions, and in 1971, he took home two gold medals—one from the Pan-American Games, and the other from the wrestling world championships.

Then the following year, all those long hours of dedicated training paid off. Despite a painful knee injury, Gable won the gold medal in the lightweight class (149 pounds) for freestyle wrestling at the Olympics in Munich. He didn't give up a single point in his six matches.

Gable retired from wrestling in 1973 and joined the University of Iowa as the assistant coach of the wrestling team. In 1977, he became head coach. The team then ran off an unbelievable nine consecutive NCAA Intercollegiate Wrestling Championships from 1978 to 1986. After a five year break, the team then won three more championships in a row from 1991-1993.

Gable also coached American teams in several international freestyle competitions. He coached the 1984 American Olympic team, which won seven gold medals. In 1985, he was inducted into the U.S. Olympic Hall of Fame.

Gable retired from coaching in 1998, having won a staggering 15 NCAA championships in his 21 years as a head coach.

Dan Gable

Before **Bobby Orr** laced on a pair of skates, hockey defensive players were supposed to do one thing, and one thing only: play defense. However, Orr showed that defensive players could be offensive threats too, and so he revolutionized the game of hockey.

Robert Gordon Orr was born in 1948, in Parry Sound, Ontario, Canada. He began playing street hockey at the tender age of four, and by the time he was in kindergarten he was already in an organized league: the Parry Sound Minor Squirt Hockey League. Showing a glimpse of future greatness, he was named the league's Most Valuable Player in the Pee Wee Division when he was nine years old.

Orr worked incessantly to perfect his hockey skills; he skated every day after school until the sun set, and only darkness put a halt to his playing. All of Orr's hard work paid off—he was just 14 when he was signed to an amateur contract by the Boston Bruins of the National Hockey League (NHL).

Orr had an outstanding career in junior hockey, then came up to the Bruins for the 1966-67 season. He won the Calder Trophy as the NHL's outstanding rookie for that season.

It didn't take him long to totally redefine the defenseman's role in hockey. Prior to Orr, defensive players had been content to remain by their goalie and assist him when the other team went on the attack. Orr showed that a defenseman could be an offensive force as well. He was a lightning-fast skater, and he thrilled fans with his headlong rushes up the ice, charging toward the other team's goalie with the puck in his possession.

In fact, Orr won the NHL's scoring title in both 1970 and 1975 —a feat usually accomplished by traditionally high scorers like wings or centers. He was the first defenseman to win the scoring crown.

Although he only played nine seasons because of knee problems, Orr piled up numerous individual honors. In 1969 and 1970 he was named the NHL's Most Valuable Player. He also won the Norris Trophy, awarded to the league's best defenseman, for eight straight seasons. Orr was a first team All-Star for eight consecutive seasons as well.

The Bruins won two Stanley Cups during Orr's tenure with them—in 1970 and 1972. Both years he won the Conn Smythe Trophy as the outstanding player in the playoffs.

Bobby Orr

Orr played his final few seasons with the Chicago Blackhawks, but by then knee injuries had reduced him to a shadow of his former self. He retired in 1979, and was elected to the NHL Hall of Fame the same year.

71. Mark Spitz
(1950-) Swimming

In the long history of the Olympic Games, no athlete had ever won seven gold medals in a single Olympics—until American swimmer **Mark Spitz** accomplished the feat in 1972.

A native of Modesto, California, it wasn't until his family moved to Sacramento when he was eight years old that Spitz began swimming competitively. He trained at the Santa Clara Swim Club as a teenager. In 1967, he set world records in the 400-meter freestyle event, and both the 100 and 200-meter butterfly events.

Mark Spitz

In 1968, Spitz created somewhat of a controversy by announcing that he'd win six medals at that year's Olympics. He fell short of his ambitious goal, however, winning just two gold medals as a member of the 4 x 100-meter and 4 x 200-meter freestyle relay teams. He also won a silver and bronze in the 100-meter butterfly race and 100-meter freestyle events. Still, it was a disappointing performance by an athlete who figured to dominate his sport. It would be another four years before that happened.

After the 1968 Olympics, Spitz entered Indiana State University. Over the next four years, he won numerous NCAA (National Collegiate Athletic Association) and AAU (Amateur Athletic Union) titles in 100, 200, and 500 yard butterfly and freestyle events. As the captain of the school's swim team, he helped it continue its run of six consecutive NCAA championships (1968-1973). In 1971, Spitz won the Sullivan Award as the top amateur athlete in the United States.

Then came the 1972 Munich Olympics, and Mark Spitz's historic hour. He set world records and won the gold medal in all four individual events that he entered. In the 100-meter freestyle, his time was a record 51.2 2 seconds. In the 200-meter freestyle, he set another record with a time of 1:52.78. He won the 100-meter butterfly competition in a record 54.27 seconds, and set a fourth record in winning the 200-meter butterfly in 2:00.07.

Spitz also won three more gold medals as a member of U.S. team which won the 400-meter freestyle relay, the 800-meter freestyle relay, and the 400-meter medley relay. The U.S. team victories in these events were also set in world record times.

After his phenomenal success at the Olympics, Spitz retired from swimming. He was greatly in demand for a time as a media personality and a spokesperson on television commercials. Twenty years after his triumphs, he attempted a comeback for the 1992 Olympics, but age had robbed him of his skills and he did not qualify for that year's Games.

In 1983, Mark Spitz became one of the first inductees in the U.S. Olympic Hall of Fame.

72. Gustavo Thoeni
(1951-) Skiing

Gustavo Thoeni is one of the greatest Alpine skiers in history.

He was born on February 28, 1951, and as a young man, he became so proficient at skiing that he was recognized as a leader of the so-called new breed of Italian Alpine skiers.

Like other members of this new breed, Thoeni's specialties were the slalom and the giant slalom, events that demand speed, agility, and a fierce competitive spirit. While the downhill race is a contest of sheer speed and cornering over a vertical course, the slalom emphasizes technical virtuosity.

The race is run over a switchback-style course, demanding quick, short turns through various combinations of gates.

In the slalom men's competition, there are 55 to 75 gates, and the length of the course is comparatively short, at 459 to 722 feet; for women, there are 40-60 gates on a course ranging from 394 to 722 feet.

In the giant slalom, the gates are fewer and farther apart, and the race is run on a longer course, from 820 to 1,312 feet for men, and 820 to 984 feet for women. Each skier races twice, and the total of both runs determines the winner.

In 1970, before he was even 20 years old, Thoeni was the leader in the World Cup giant slalom standings. The following year, he won his first overall World Cup title—the first of four that he would capture. He was the first Italian skier to be an overall World Cup champion.

Thoeni had perhaps his greatest year in 1972. He won the overall World Cup title again, and was again the leader in the giant slalom rankings. However, his biggest triumph that year came at the Winter Olympic Games in Sapporo, Japan. He won a gold medal in the giant slalom, and a silver medal in the slalom.

The following year, Thoeni won his third consecutive overall World Cup title. After missing out on the overall title in 1974, Thoeni again captured the crown in 1975, concluding a remarkable streak of four World Cup titles in five years. Thoeni was again prominent at the next Olympics in 1976, winning his second silver medal in the slalom at Innsbruck, Austria.

In addition to his World Cup victories, Thoeni won two FIS World Alpine Ski Championships at the legendary ski slopes of St. Moritz in 1974, for the slalom and giant slalom.

After his retirement from competitive skiing in the late 1970s, Thoeni became a coach. He had the pleasure of seeing one of his pupils, the great **Alberto Tomba**, also become a champion international skier.

Gustavo Thoeni

73. Nikolai Andrianov
(1952-) Gymnastics

One of the greatest athletes ever to emerge from the Soviet Union, **Nikolai Andrianov** is also one of the few people in Olympic history to win seven gold medals.

Born on October 14, 1952, Andrianov showed so much gymnastic aptitude as a child that he was placed into the Soviet system for that sport at an early age. (At this time in the Soviet Union, any child who showed skill in any type of athletic endeavor was directed toward that sport as a youngster.)

By the time of the 1972 Olympic Games in Munich, Gemany, Andrianov was ready to demonstrate his astounding ability to the world. He won a gold medal in the floor exercise with a score of 19.175 points, beating out two strong Japanese competitors, **Akinori Nakayama** and **Shigeru Kasamatsu**, who won the silver and bronze medals, respectively. Adrianov also won a bronze medal in the long horse vault event that year.

By 1976, the Soviet men's gymnastics team, as well as teams from other Eastern bloc countries, were poised to break the dominance of the Japanese men's team As one of the leaders of the Soviet team, Andrianov led the charge.

In the Games in Montreal that year, Andrianov won the gold medal in the all-around competition with 116.65 points, beating the two-time defending Olympic champion, the great Japanese gymnast **Sawao Kato** (see no. 66). The Soviet gymnast also won three other gold medals that year—in the long horse vault (19.45 points), the rings (19.65 points), and the floor exercise (19.45 points).

Rounding out his collection of medal winning performances that year, Andrianov won a silver in the parallel bars and a bronze in the pommel horse. Although Japan won the gold in the team combined exercises for the fifth straight Olympics, Andrianov had helped stamp the Soviets as the rising power in gymnastics.

In 1980, it all came together for the Soviet team at the Olympics they hosted in Moscow. The Soviets won the gold in the team combined event, and Andrianov took the gold in the long horse vault competition. In addition, **Aleksandr Dityatin** won gold medals for the all-around competition and the rings, and **Aleksandr Tkachyav** took the gold in the parallel bars.

With his participation in three Olympics, Adrianov holds the career record for most medals won with 15, as well as being in the elite group of athletes who have won seven gold medals.

Nikolai Andrianov

74. Jimmy Connors
(1952-) Tennis

One of the top tennis players in the world during the 1970s and 1980s, **Jimmy Connors** led a new wave of feisty and aggressive players that dominated the sport's professional ranks.

Connors was born in Belleville, Illinois in 1952. An apocryphal story of his childhood is that by his third birthday, his mother Gloria had put a tennis racquet in his hands and had him practicing. What is known to be true is that his mother was a professional tennis instructor who taught him the game. She also instilled in him the aggressiveness that marked his playing career.

When Connors was a teenager, his family moved to California so he could receive expert training and coaching from tennis greats **Pancho Gonzales** and **Pancho Segura**. While attending college at UCLA, Connors won the National Collegiate Athletic Association (NCAA) men's singles title in 1971. After turning professional in 1972, Connors won his first two tournaments.

However, his breakout year professionally, came in 1974. He won three of four grand slam tournaments that year—the Australian Open, Wimbledon, and the U.S. Open. He was banned from playing in the French Open, the fourth grand slam tournament, because of a prior contract he had signed to play in the professional World Team Tennis league.

Connors was the leader of a new type of tennis player—highly volatile, criticizing and even cursing linesmen, and arguing continually over lost points. His behavior was the complete opposite of the quiet, genteel prototype of the traditional tennis player. Among those who played tennis in this aggressive manner were the sharp-tempered Romanian, **Ilie Nastase**, and American **John McEnroe**.

Connors matched his personality and behavior with an aggressive style of tennis. A left-hander who used a two-handed backhand, Connors was known for his relentless manner on the court. An opponent once said of him, "Playing him is like fighting **Joe Frazier**. The guy's always coming at you. He never lets up."

Jimmy Connors

Connors won five U.S. Open titles and two Wimbledon championships during his career. He also set all-time records by winning 84 Wimbledon matches and 98 U.S. Open matches. His 109 career wins in professional singles championship matches is another record.

As he aged, the once-abrasive Connors mellowed, behaving more graciously on and off the court and winning over many tennis fans who had once disliked him. He was among the top ten in rankings until 1988. He then retired, but made a strong comeback in 1991, beating much younger opponents and making it all the way to the semifinals of the U.S. Open.

In 1993, Connors helped found a seniors tour for players who were at least 35 years of age.

75. Annemarie Moser-Proell
(1953-) Skiing

Annemarie Moser-Proell won six World Cup titles during the 1970s, more than any other skier at the time—and she never had a skiing lesson in her life.

As a child in Kleinarl, Salzburg, Austria, Moser grew up in the Alps. She made her own skis when she was four years old, and began teaching herself to ski. However, unlike many others who excel in a particular sport and go on to study with a teacher, Moser never had a professional lesson. Instead she developed her own techniques and mastery of the slopes.

She learned quickly and well. When she was 15 years old, she became a member of the Austrian national ski team. Although she was superb in all three racing events—the downhill, the giant slalom, and the slalom—it was the downhill on which she focused her energies.

Moser was the youngest skier to ever win the World Cup overall championship when she won it during the 1970-71 season. She then won this title four more years in a row, and a sixth time later in the decade. She also won the World Cup giant slalom three times (1971, 1972, and 1975). Demonstrating her dominance in the downhill, she won the Women's World Cup downhill championship an all-time record of seven times.

Moser didn't ignore the Olympics. At the 1972 Games in Sapporo, Japan, she won silver medals in the giant slalom and downhill events.

Moser got married between the 1973 and 1974 seasons, but that didn't slow her down in the least. She continued to ski competitively—and win. She set an all-time mark by recording 33 wins in World Cup downhill events. She also finished second in lifetime wins in the World Cup giant slalom and World Cup combined events.

Moser-Proll retired at the conclusion of the 1974-1975 skiing season. However, she returned to the competitive arena in 1978, and won her sixth World Cup title. Capping off a brilliant career, she won a gold medal in the downhill event at the 1980 Winter Olympics.

Annemarie Moser-Proell

76. Raisa Smetanina
(1953-) Skiing

Raisa Smetanina had an Olympic career of incredible success and longevity. In a competition that is usually reserved for the youngest and the strongest, the Soviet skier won 10 medals over five Olympics—a period of 20 years.

Smetanina began her remarkable "medal run" at the 1976 Olympics at Innsbruck, Austria. She won a gold medal in the women's 10-kilometer cross-country skiing event, and a silver in the 5-kilometer cross-country competition. Both were tight contests with **Helena Takalo** of Finland. That year, Smetanina won another gold as part of the first place Soviet women's 20-kilometer relay team.

In the 1980 Lake Placid, New York Olympic Games she picked right up where she left off four years earlier. She won a gold in the women's 5-kilometer cross-country race, defeating **Hikka Riihivuori** of Finland, who won the silver. Smetanina also won a silver medal as a member of the USSR's women's 20-kilometer relay team.

Four years later, Smetanina won two silver medals at the Olympics in Sarajevo—one in the women's 10-kilometer cross-country race, and another in the women's 20-kilometer cross-country event. In both events, she was beaten for the gold by **Marja-Liisa Hamalainen**, of Finland.

In the 1988 Games in Calgary, Canada, Smetanina won two more medals: a silver in the 10-kilometer race, and a bronze in the 20-kilometer race. She then picked up her record tenth medal at the 1992 Games in Albertville, France, winning a gold as part of the women's 20-kilometer relay team playing under a banner called the Unified Team, made up of former Soviet Union republics.

After Smetanina won her tenth medal she retired, having set a record in Nordic skiing that will be hard to match.

Raisa Smetanina

77. Walter Payton
(1954-1999) Football

Walter Payton

A gentle, friendly man off the field, but a terror on it, **Walter Payton** was perhaps the greatest all-around running back in the history of the National Football League.

Payton was born in Columbia, Mississippi. He attended college at Jackson State University, where he set a college football record for points scored. When he graduated in 1975, the NFL's Chicago Bears drafted him, whereupon he set another record—his contract was the richest ever given to a rookie.

Payton quickly proved that he was worth it. After rushing for 679 yards in his first year, he ran for at least 1,200 yards in 10 out of the next 11 seasons. Beginning in 1976, he led the league's National Football Conference in

rushing for the first of five straight years—and was named to the Pro Bowl for the first of nine times. The following year he ran for a career-high 1,852 yards and scored 14 touchdowns, helping the Bears make the playoffs for the first time in 14 years.

In 1977, Payton ran for a then-record 275 yards in a single game, and finished the year with an average yards per carry of 5.5. He was voted the NFL's MVP that year, the first of two times he was to receive that honor.

Payton was the league's MVP once again in the 1985 season, when he ran for more than 1,500 yards. The Bears were the best team in football that year, posting a record of 15-1 and winning the 1986 Super Bowl.

Despite the tremendous physical punishment that NFL running backs receive, Payton missed just one game during his 13-year career. He credited that to a rigorous off-season training regimen that included running up steep hills near his home. That undoubtedly contributed to his incredible leg strength. Time and again on the football field, Payton would seem trapped by a defender, only to stick out a leg and then yank it free from the grasp of a tackler. In contrast to his toughness as a player, Payton had a gentle, kind nature, and was nicknamed **Sweetness** by his teammates.

Payton retired after the 1987 season. At that time, he was the NFL's leading rusher, with 16,726 yards. (That record was broken by **Emmitt Smith** of the Dallas Cowboys in 2002.) During his career, Payton also had 492 pass receptions for 4,538 yards, bringing his combined yardage total to 21,264. He also scored 125 touchdowns—110 of them rushing.

In 1993, Payton was inducted into the pro football Hall of Fame. He died in 1999 of a liver ailment.

One of the most successful and popular women's tennis players in history, **Chris Evert** won 18 grand slam singles championships, third on the all-time list.

She was born in Fort Lauderdale, Florida, and grew up in a family in which tennis was a passion. Her parents and four siblings were all dedicated players. The kids won competitions, and their father was the coach.

Evert got her first racquet when she was five, and developed a dedicated practice routine as a child. She entered every age group competition available, so that by the time she was 12 years old, she was ranked number two in the United States for that age group. At age 16, she was ranked number one nationally.

When she was 16 years old, she won 46 straight matches. Then she debuted at the U.S. Open in Forest Hills and made it all the way to the semifinals, becoming the youngest woman in history to do so. At age 17, she won the $100,000 Virginia Slims Tournament at Boca Raton—the richest women's tournament at the time.

Evert turned pro in 1973, and won six of seven tournaments she entered. She won 15 tournaments in her second pro year, including Wimbledon, the Canadian Open, and the French Open. In 1974, she was the Associated Press Woman Athlete of the Year. The following year, she was ranked Number One, and won her first U.S. Open title.

Evert was at her best in grand slam events. She won the U.S. Open four years in row (1975-1978), and then again in 1980 and 1982. She was a finalist at the French Open ten years in a row (1973-1982), winning the title seven times. With her three Wimbledon crowns, and two Australian Open titles, she had a total of 18 grand slam singles championships, which ranks her third behind **Margaret Smith Court** (see no. 63) and **Helen Wills Moody** (see no. 24.)

One of the first players to use a two-handed backhand, Evert was never flashy, but was steady and consistent. She was also nearly unflappable on the court, earning the nickname **Little Miss Icicle** for her demeanor during matches.

Evert also made some headlines during her career with her romance with fellow American tennis star **Jimmy Connors** during the 1970s. She married British tennis star **John Lloyd** in 1979, but they divorced in 1987. She married former American Olympic skier **Andy Mill** in 1988.

Evert retired in 1990, while still near the top of her game. In 1995, she was unanimously voted into the International Tennis Hall of Fame.

Chris Evert

Bernard Hinault
(1954-) Cycling

One of the greatest cyclists in history, **Bernard Hinault** won the Tour de France five times.

Hinault was born in 1954 on the northern coast of Bretagne, France; as a youth, he rode his bike at least 15 miles every day. After four years of training as a runner, he watched his cousin win a bicycle race in 1971, and decided that he wanted to try racing as well. Borrowing his brother's bike, he rode it to victory in his first race. From then on he was hooked; he won 12 of the 20 events he entered in 1971. The following year, he won the French national junior championship.

Bernard Hinault

Following a stint in the military that did not afford him any bike-riding opportunities, Hinault returned to the sport and quickly became one of its dominant athletes. He won 13 races, including the national pursuit championship, in 1974.

Turning pro in 1974, Hinault became known as the **Badger** because of his cool, calculating racing personality and aggressive riding style. During the 1970s and 80s, he won almost every European cycling event, including the Tours of Spain in 1978 and 1983, the Tours of Italy in 1980, 1982, and 1985, and

the world championship road race.

However, the "Super Bowl" of bike racing is the Tour de France, and Hinault was prepared for it. He first won the event in 1978, with a time of 108 hours and 18 minutes. The following year he won it again. The race totaled 2,200 miles and took nearly a month to complete. Hinault won it with a time of 103:06.50.

In 1980, he had to drop out of the race with tendinitis, but in 1981 he was healthy again, and he won the race for a third time, with a time of 96:19.38.

Typical of Hinault's riding personality was his victory in the 1982 Tour de France. The distance was 2,181 miles, with the cyclists covering it in increments of about 100 miles. Hinault staged a dramatic, come-from-behind charge in the last stage of the race to overtake the leader and win the event for the fourth time. His fifth victory came in 1985.

Hinault's outspoken and confident manner made him a hero throughout France, and elevated the sport of cycling to new heights of popularity. When he retired in 1986, Hinault had 194 professional victories to his credit. That year he was voted the Top French Athlete of the Last 60 Years.

80. Larry Bird
(1956-) Basketball

Larry Bird not only helped revitalize a historic pro basketball franchise that had fallen on hard times, but he injected new life into the entire National Basketball Association.

Bird was born in the Indiana town of French Lick, and after starring on his high school team, he attended Indiana State University on a scholarship. In his senior year in 1979, Bird was named the collegiate player of the year as he led the team to an undefeated regular season, and took them all the way to the NCAA championship game, where they lost to a Michigan State team led by **Magic Johnson** (see no. 86).

Bird was drafted as a forward by the once-mighty Boston Celtics, who had fallen on hard times in the late 70s. Bird had an immediate impact on the Celtics, leading them to a first place finish in their division in 1980. He was named the NBA's Rookie of the Year that season.

The following year, Bird led the Celtics to the NBA championship. Boston won two more titles during Bird's career, in 1984 and 1986; both times, he was voted the Most Valuable Player in the playoffs. Bird was also named the league's MVP for three straight years, 1984–1986.

In the 1986-87 season, Bird became the first player in basketball history to shoot at least .500 from the floor and at least .900 from the free throw line. One of the best shooting forwards in NBA history, he was also a superb passer, often getting the ball to a teammate without looking in his direction.

Along with Magic Johnson of the Los Angeles Lakers, Bird was credited with renewing fan interest in the NBA. The league had been struggling before his arrival; ticket sales were down, there were no real marquee players, and fan interest was waning. However, Bird changed all that with his dynamic play. He and Johnson maintained a spirited but friendly rivalry throughout the 1980s, as they dueled on the court, and their teams battled for the league championship on several occasions.

A bad back hastened Bird's retirement before the 1992-93 NBA season, just after he had won a gold medal as a member of the U.S. Olympic Basketball Team. He left the game with lifetime totals of 21,791 points (a 24.3 average per game), 8,974 rebounds, and an .886 free throw shooting percentage.

After his retirement, Bird became the coach of the NBA's Indiana Pacers. He led the team to the playoffs several times, but could not get into the championship round. In 1998, he was elected to the basketball Hall of Fame.

Larry Bird

Sugar Ray Leonard
(1956-) Boxing

Sugar Ray Leonard

Ray Leonard was one of the greatest boxers of his era, and the first prizefighter to win titles in five different weight classes.

Born in Wilmington, North Carolina, he was named Ray Charles by his mother, who wanted him to be a singer; instead, after he became a successful prizefighter, he got the nickname **Sugar Ray**, after the famous boxer of the 1940s and 50s, **Sugar Ray Robinson**.

As an amateur, Leonard compiled an amazing record of 145-5 with 75 knockouts. He won the National Golden Gloves, two international championships, and two gold medals as a light welterweight—one at the 1975 Pan-American Games, and another at the 1976 Montreal Olympics.

Leonard's plan was to retire from boxing after the Olympics, but family financial needs changed his thinking. He turned pro in 1977.

Two years later, he defeated **Wilfredo Benitez** to win the World Boxing Council (WBC) welterweight crown, only to lose it to **Roberto Duran** in 1980. The rematch held later that year was one of the most famous boxing matches in history. Duran, who had a reputation as a tough guy, suddenly lowered his hands during the 8th round, cried out *"No mas!"* in Spanish (No more!), and walked back to his corner, although he seemed unhurt.

In 1981, Leonard won the World Boxing Association (WBA) welterweight title from **Tommy "Hit Man" Hearns**, as well as the WBA junior middleweight championship by knocking out **Ayub Kalue**.

Leonard was a champion for the ages—a fighter who had the punching power of a mule kick, and the speed and agility of a ballet dancer. In addition, he was an extremely intelligent and photogenic man—perfect for television. This combination of ability and good looks propelled him to great popularity.

It seemed as if he would dominate his weight classes for a long time, but in 1982 a freak eye injury—a detached retina—forced his premature retirement from the ring.

Leonard returned to the ring for one fight in 1984, and then retired again. However, he returned again in 1987, moving up in weight class, and winning the WBC middleweight title from **Marvin Hagler**. The next year, he won the WBC light heavyweight and super middleweight titles, making him the first boxer to win titles in five different weight classes.

However, Leonard was not quite the same devastating fighter he had been before his eye injury. After losing a bout in 1991, he didn't fight again for six years. In 1997, he returned to the ring, but lost and then quit boxing for good. In 1997 he was inducted into the International Boxing Hall of Fame.

82. Joe Montana
(1956-) Football

Joe Montana was one of the greatest quarterbacks in the history of the National Football League, leading the San Francisco 49ers to four Super Bowl titles.

A native of Monogahela, Pennsylvania, Montana went to college at Notre Dame University. There he quickly gained a national reputation as a pinpoint passer and outstanding field general. He won particular acclaim for his ability to bring his team from behind, most famously in the 1979 Cotton Bowl; in that game, he rallied Notre Dame from a 23-point deficit in the fourth quarter to defeat the University of Houston, 35-34.

Drafted by the NFL's San Francisco 49ers in 1979, Montana quickly lifted that team from the depths of obscurity to one of the most dominant in league history. Montana became the starting quarterback in his second season, and led the league with a 64.5 completion percentage. The next season, he quarterbacked the 49ers into the playoffs and then led them to a 26-21 victory over the Cincinnati Bengals in the 1982 Super Bowl. In that game, he was 14 for 22 in passing for 157 yards and one touchdown. He also scored another touchdown rushing, and was voted the game's MVP.

In 1985, Montana got the team to the Super Bowl again, where they defeated the Miami Dolphins 38-16. Once more Montana was brilliant in the game, completing 24 of 35 passes for 331 yards and two touchdowns. He was again voted the game's MVP.

With Montana at the helm, the 49ers won the Super Bowl again in 1989 and 1990. In the 1989 game, a rematch against the Bengals, Montana engineered one of his famous "comeback" drives, taking the 49ers 92 yards in the game's final two minutes to squeak out a 20-16 victory. In 1990, Montana simply took apart a good Denver

Broncos squad. He completed 22 passes in 29 attempts, for 297 yards and five touchdowns as the 49ers cruised to victory, 55-10. Montana was once again the game's MVP, becoming the first three-time winner of the award.

Montana played his final two seasons with the Kansas City Chiefs, but could not repeat his magic with them and the team never made it to the Super Bowl.

Montana retired after the 1994 season. For his career, he had an incredible 93.5 quarterback rating, was third in career completions with 2,929, fifth in career passing yardage with 35,124, and sixth in career touchdown passes with 244. He led the NFL in passing five times, and was named to the Pro Bowl eight times.

In 2000, he was inducted into the pro football Hall of Fame.

Joe Montana

89

No discussion of great tennis players can occur without bringing up the name of **Martina Navratilova**, one of the best players ever to pick up a racquet.

She was born in Prague, Czechoslovakia. Her parents had an unhappy marriage, and they got divorced when she was three; her father died tragically six years later. Her mother loved to play tennis, and often took Martina to the courts with her. In 1961, her mother married **Mike Navratil**, and Martina's name became Navratilova when she added the Czech suffix for "daughter of." Navratil taught his stepdaughter to play tennis, and when he took her to see **Rod Laver** play in a tournament, she decided then and there that she wanted to become a tennis player.

At the age of eight, Navratilova competed in her first tournament and made the semifinals. The next year, she began practicing under the watchful eye of **George Parma**, the great Czech tennis coach.

By the time she was 14 years old, Navratilova had won the National Championship for her age group. Three years later, she was her country's number one woman player, with three National Women's championships and the National Junior championship to her credit.

However, Navratilova was growing increasingly frustrated by the Czechoslovakian Tennis Federation's interference with her

career. Finally in 1975, while playing in the U.S. Open, she asked for political asylum and defected to America.

Now her brilliant career kicked into high gear. In 1975, she and partner **Chris Evert** won the French Open doubles championship, and then the following year they took the Wimbledon doubles championship.

By the late 1970s, Navratilova began to dominate Wimbledon in singles play. She won the tournament in 1978 and 1979, and then six years in a row from 1982 through 1987. In 1990, she won it again, giving her an amazing nine Wimbledon titles.

Navratilova held the top ranking in the world for all but 22 weeks of a five-year, 282-week period from 1982 to 1987. During the 1980s, she won four U.S. Opens, three Australian Opens, and two French Opens.

Navratilova proved to be just as good at doubles tennis as she was at singles. She won 31 women's doubles titles in grand slam events, many of them playing with **Pam Shriver**. Although she retired from singles competition in the early 1990s, Navratilova was still going strong in doubles competition in 2003. At the age of 46, she won the Australian Open mixed doubles championship, becoming the oldest person to win a grand slam event. It was her 57th grand slam title, second all-time to the 62 won by **Margaret Smith Court**.

Martina Navratilova

84. Eric Heiden
(1958-) Speed Skating

Eric Heiden was a unique athlete and individual. He accomplished the unprecedented feat of winning five individual gold medals in the Olympics. Then after the victories, he walked away from his sport, turning his back on fame and a potential for huge financial gain.

A native of Madison, Wisconsin, Heiden began skating at the age of two. As he grew older, he added running, cycling, and weightlifting to his training regimen. When he was a teenager, Heiden began training as a speed skater with his sister Beth, who would also go on to participate in the Olympics.

In 1976, Heiden was on the cusp of greatness. He participated in the Olympic games at Innsbruck, Austria that year, but he did not win a medal. He also finished fifth in the world speed skating championships.

That proved to be Heiden's "warm-up" year. In 1977, at the age of 18, Heiden won the world junior overall, senior overall, and sprint speed-skating championships— which was an unprecedented sweep. His victory was the first ever by an American in the event.

Heiden continued his dominance of the world championships over the next three years. He swept all three championships in 1978, and won both the sprint and overall titles again in 1979 and 1980. Along the way, he set new world records in the 10,000 meter race (1979) and the 1,000 and 1,500 meter races (1980).

However, Heiden's biggest triumphs came at the 1980 Winter Olympic Games in Lake Placid, New York. He won an incredible five gold medals for his individual performance in the speed skating events. It was the only time in Olympic history anyone has ever won five gold medals for individual events. In the process, Heiden set two world records and three Olympic records.

Eric Heiden

Heiden simply dominated every speed skating event, from the sprints to the endurance races. His victories and record-setting times were: 500-meter, 38.03 seconds; 1,000-meter, 1:15.18; 1,500-meter, 1:55.44; 5,000-meter, 7:02.29; and the 10,000-meter, 14.28.13. His victories in the 500 and 10,000 meter races were set in world record times, while he set new Olympic records in the other three events.

For his landmark performance, Heiden received the Sullivan Award as the top American amateur athlete of 1980. After the Olympics, Heiden announced his retirement, and although commercial endorsements were showered upon him, he refused them.

Heiden later became a competitive cyclist, but his career in the athletic spotlight ended after the 1980 Olympics. He summed up his view on fame and stardom right after his retirement when he said, "I really liked it best when I was a nobody."

85. **Florence Griffith-Joyner**
(1959-1998) Track and Field

With her athletic ability, exuberant attitude, and wildly-colored attire **Florence Griffith-Joyner** captured the hearts of a generation. Only her untimely death prevented her from reaching greater heights of popularity.

Born in Los Angeles, Florence Griffith began running track at age seven, and won the Jesse Owens National Youth Games at 14 years old. She set records in sprinting and the long jump at Jordan High School, and then

Florence Griffith-Joyner

enrolled at California State University to train under famed track coach **Bob Kersee**.

When Kersee moved to the University of California at Los Angeles (UCLA) so did Griffith. She was the National Collegiate Athletic Association 200-meter champion in 1982, and then won the NCAA 400-meter in 1983. After winning a silver medal in the 1984 Olympics in the 200-meter dash, she went into semiretirement.

In 1987 she married **Al Joyner**, an Olympic gold medalist and the brother of track star **Jackie Joyner-Kersee**, who was the wife of Griffith's coach. That year Griffith also re-emerged into the track-and-field spotlight by winning the 200-meter dash at the world championship games in Rome, and finishing second overall in the competition.

However, 1988 was to be the year of Flo-Jo, as she came to be known. In the Olympic trials on July 16, she set a 100-meter record of 10.49, a full quarter-second off the previous

mark. No one in history had beaten an existing 100-meter record by more than one-tenth of a second up to that point. The following day, she set a U.S. record for the 200-meter run at 21.77 seconds.

Primed and ready for the Olympics, Flo-Jo won three gold medals in the Games in Seoul, Korea. She won the individual 100-and 200-meter races, and was a member of the winning 400-meter relay team. She also won a silver medal in the 1,600-meter relay.

With her Olympic triumphs came a host of awards. She was named Sportswoman of the Year in France and the Athlete of the Year by the Soviet news agency TASS. In 1989, she won the U.S. Olympic Committee Award, Berlin's Golden Camera Award, the Sullivan Award as the top American amateur athlete, and the Jesse Owens Award as the outstanding track and field athlete of the year.

Flo-Jo's one-legged running suits, designer running shoes, and long, multicolored fingernails made her a sensation with the media and young sports fans; soon she had a number of lucrative business enterprises going, including fashion design, writing, and acting.

In 1989, she announced her retirement from track to attend to her outside interests. In September 1998, she died of suffocation in her sleep after suffering an epileptic fit. She was just 38 years old.

92

The engaging smile and upbeat personality of **Earvin "Magic" Johnson** masked a fierce competitive spirit and a drive to win that helped the Los Angeles Lakers garner five National Basketball Association championships in the 1980s.

Johnson acquired the nickname Magic after a magnificent high school game in his hometown of Lansing, Michigan, in which he scored 36 points, had 18 rebounds, and dished out 16 assists. Playing point guard as a sophomore for Michigan State University, Johnson led the school in a victorious effort against **Larry Bird's** Indiana State University for the 1979 NCAA championship. The Bird-Johnson rivalry would continue throughout the 1980s as both players moved into the professional ranks.

Leaving college after that year, Johnson joined the Los Angeles Lakers of the NBA. His playmaking ability, combined with his high-grade enthusiasm, were the added ingredients the Lakers needed to reach the championship heights. Along with **Kareem Abdul - Jabbar**, Johnson sparked the Lakers immediately that season and they won the 1980 championship. With Johnson running the Lakers high-powered "Showtime" offense, the Lakers the won four more NBA titles in the 1980s—in 1982, 1985, 1987, and 1988.

Johnson was considered one of the greatest point guards and playmakers in NBA history, piling up numerous individual honors. In 1980, he was the first rookie to be named MVP of the NBA championship finals. He was the league championship series MVP twice more (1982 and 1987), and was the NBA's Most Valuable Player three times (1987, 1989, and 1990).

Along with the Boston Celtics' Larry Bird, Johnson is credited with revitalizing interest in the NBA. The Bird-Johnson,

Celtics-Lakers duels on the court were exciting to watch. In particular, Johnson's magnetic smile and enthusiastic personality were always in demand by the television networks, which helped the NBA gain even more exposure.

Johnson stunned the sports world in late 1991 when he announced that he had tested positive for the AIDS virus and was retiring from basketball. However, he played on the 1992 U.S. Olympic basketball team—the Dream Team—that won a gold medal. He then announced that he would return to the Lakers, and began the 1992 NBA season with the team. However, his return caused a controversy, and he subsequently retired again after a few months.

In the closing months of the 1993-1994 season, Johnson became head coach of the Lakers. However, he didn't stay in the position long, citing frustration with the players' attitudes. Then, in another stunning turnaround, Johnson returned to the Lakers as a player for the 1996 season. When the team was eliminated in the first round of the playoffs, Johnson retired for the final time.

Magic Johnson

87. Diego Maradona
(1960-) Soccer

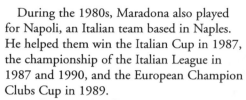

As a soccer player, he wanted to do for Argentina what **Pelé** had done for Brazil. However, although **Diego Maradona** scaled the heights of superstardom, he could not defeat the personal demons inside of him.

He was born Diego Armando Maradona in Lanus near Buenos Aires, the fifth of eight children. He began playing soccer for an Argentinian youth team when he was nine. At the age of 16, he became the youngest member of Argentina's national team. Although Maradona was a star in his country by 1978, he was left off the national team that year — the coach did not think he could handle the pressure of World Cup competition—and did not participate in Argentina's World Cup victory.

The following year, however, he was voted South American Player of the Year. From 1982 to 1984 he played for the Barcelona team in Spain. Maradona then led Argentina back to the World Cup and victory again in 1986. He was the most dominant player in the tournament that year, and was voted the MVP of the event.

During the 1980s, Maradona also played for Napoli, an Italian team based in Naples. He helped them win the Italian Cup in 1987, the championship of the Italian League in 1987 and 1990, and the European Champion Clubs Cup in 1989.

At the pinnacle of his career, however, in March 1991, Maradona sabotaged it all by being accused of drug use. He was dropped from the Naples team and suspended from international competition for 15 months while he faced drug charges in Argentina.

In September 1992, Maradona seemed to be on the comeback trail, signing with Sevilla, a Spanish team. But he was a shell of his former self, and was dropped by the team after one season.

Maradona said that the reason he struggled so mightily with Sevilla was that the training sessions were too much for him. He subsequently returned to Argentina for another comeback. However, during the World Cup of 1994 he was again suspended for 15 months, this time testing positive for using ephedrine, a banned substance.

Maradona became the coach of Racing Club, a soccer team from Argentina, but he quit in mid-1995. He then returned to playing, this time with the Boca Juniors team from Buenos Aires, before retiring for good in 1997. He served as a TV commentator in Argentina during the World Cup in 1998.

Despite his numerous problems that most certainly shortened his career, Maradona remained one of the most popular soccer players in the history of the sport. In 2000, he was voted FIFA "best football player of the century" in a worldwide poll on the internet.

Diego Maradona

Greg Louganis was the first male diver in more than 50 years to win both the platform and the springboard events in the same Olympics. He then repeated those feats four years later, becoming the only male diver in the long history of the Olympic Games to win those events twice in succession.

Born to Samoan and Swedish parents, Louganis was given up for adoption by his teenage mother shortly after his birth. Raised in El Cajon, in southern California, he had a difficult childhood. He was extremely shy as a youngster, primarily because of a reading disability, and classmates often hurled racial insults at him because of his dark skin.

However, Louganis found solace in dance classes, which he and his sister joined almost as soon as they could walk. In grade school Louganis added gymnastics to his list of activities, and progressed to diving. When he began doing gymnastic flips off the family diving board, his stepfather enrolled him in diving class.

At the age of 11, he scored a perfect 10 in the Amateur Athletic Union (AAU) Junior Olympics. Then Louganis came under the tutelage of former Olympic diving gold medalist, Dr. Sammy Lee. When he was 16, Louganis participated in the 1976 Olympics, and won a silver medal in platform diving.

By the spring of 1978, Louganis was emerging as a premier diver. That year he won the world platform championship and the AAU indoor 1-meter and 3-meter titles. The next year, he won gold medals in both the springboard and the platform events at the Pan-American Games.

It appeared as if Louganis was primed and ready for the 1980 Olympics, but the United States boycotted the Moscow Games, and the dreams of all the athletes, including Louganis, were put on hold. After attending the University of Miami for three years, in 1981 he switched colleges to get his Bachelor's Degree in Drama from the University of California at Irvine, and to study under diving great Ron O'Brien.

Greg Louganis

In 1982, Louganis won both the platform and springboard diving events at the world championships. Two years later, at the Los Angeles Olympics, Louganis shined, winning gold medals in both diving events. He later won the Sullivan Award as the outstanding amateur athlete in America that year.

Louganis repeated his double gold medal performance three more times—at the 1986 world championships, the 1987 Pan-American Games, and finally at the 1988 Olympics, securing his reputation as the greatest male diving champion in Olympics history.

After the 1988 Games, Louganis retired from competitive diving. In 1985, he was inducted into the U.S. Olympic Hall of Fame.

Nadia Comaneci
(1961-) Gymnastics

Nadia Comaneci

The first gymnast in Olympic history to score perfect 10.0s, tiny but mighty **Nadia Comaneci** won the hearts and minds of the sports world with her performance at the 1976 Olympics.

Comaneci was born in 1961 in Onesti, Romania. She began gymnastic training early in life. When she was six years old, the great Romanian gymnastics teacher **Bela Karoli** spotted her while he was scouting public schools for potential members of the national junior gymnastics team.

In 1969, Comaneci entered national competition. The following year she won the national junior championship. Karoli had coached her well. She continued winning competitions in her age group until 1975, when she began senior competition. That year

she entered the European championships and totally outclassed the competition, walking away with four of the five gold medals.

Despite her successes, however, Comaneci was still a well-kept secret of the Eastern Communist bloc. That changed in 1976, when she came to North America for the first time in preparation for the Olympics at Montreal, Canada. In the qualifying meets for the Games, she registered perfect scores of 10.0 six out of eight times. She then won the American Cup competition, earning several more tens along the way. She was just 15 years old, and the talk of the sports world. Everybody loved the little girl with the graceful athleticism and flawless technique.

Then came the Olympics, where she became the first gymnast to receive a perfect score from the judges, earning all 10.0s in the uneven bars event. She also won a gold medal in the all-around, and in the balance beam, where she had a near-perfect point total of 19.95. In addition, she won a bronze medal in the floor exercise, and she led Romania to the silver medal in the team competition.

In the 1980 Olympics, Comaneci repeated her triumphs. She won gold medals in the balance beam and floor exercise events, and a silver in the all-around.

Comaneci defected from Romania to the United States on November 1, 1989. In 1996, she married American gymnast **Bart Conner**.

90. Wayne Gretzky
(1961-) Hockey

They called **Wayne Gretzky** the **"Great One,"** and why not? During his 20-year National Hockey League career, he set more than 60 scoring records. He is perhaps the greatest hockey player who ever laced up a pair of skates.

Born in 1961, Gretzky was skating at the age of three on a backyard rink in his Brantford, Ontario, Canada home. His dad drilled him in the essentials of hockey, and did a good job of it; when Gretzky was 6, he was competing against 10-year-olds.

During the 1977-78 season, Gretzky played junior hockey with the Sault Sainte Marie Greyhounds of the Ontario Hockey League. Even though he was only a teenager, he scored 70 goals and had 122 assists in just 64 games.

In 1978, a few months shy of his 18th birthday, Gretzky signed a professional contract with the Indianapolis Racers of the World Hockey Association (WHA). He was the youngest athlete in North America to play on a major pro sports team. After eight games, the financially struggling Racers sold his contract to the WHA's Edmonton Oilers. Gretzky had an outstanding season for the Oilers, scoring 46 goals, adding 64 assists and being named the league's Rookie of the Year.

When the WHA folded and the Oilers moved to the NHL the following season, Gretzky became an immediate star. He amassed an amazing 137 points on 51 goals, and 86 assists, winning the first of eight straight scoring titles.

However, Gretzky was just warming up. The following season, he set an NHL scoring record with 164 points. In the 1981-82 season, he became the first player in NHL history to break the 200-point barrier when he tallied 120 assists and a record 92 goals for a total of 212 points.

Led by Gretzky, Edmonton became the NHL's most dominant team during the 1980s, winning four Stanley Cups during the decade; for his part, Gretzky won eight straight Most Valuable Player awards during that period.

Despite their championships, however, by the late 1980s the Oilers were in financial difficulty, and in 1988 they traded Gretzky to the Los Angeles Kings. His presence immediately turned them from a weak franchise into a successful one, and although he was never able to bring a Stanley Cup to L.A., Gretzky is credited with saving hockey in that city.

When he retired at the end of the 1998-99 season, Gretzky held so many NHL records it was hard to keep track of them all. Chief among them were career marks in goals (894), assists (1,963), and points (2,857). The NHL fittingly retired Gretzky's jersey number 99, meaning no other player will ever wear it.

Wayne Gretzky

American **Greg LeMond** was a three-time winner of the prestigious Tour de France cycling race in an era when it was an accomplishment just having an American in the race.

LeMond was born in Los Angeles, but his family moved to northwestern Nevada when he was a boy. There his father developed an avid interest in long-distance cycling. Soon father and son were going on cycling trips together.

In 1975, LeMond joined the Reno, Nevada Wheelman cycling club; in February 1976, he finished second in a 25-mile race. In his first few months of competition, he won 11 races in his age group, then petitioned to be allowed to compete with 16 to 19-year-olds. By year's end, he had won the Nevada Junior championship and placed fourth in the Nationals for Juniors.

From that time on, LeMond devoted himself totally to cycling. He won the gold medal in the Junior Nationals in 1977, but it was in 1978 that LeMond stamped himself as an up-and-comer in the cycling world. That year he won a gold, silver, and bronze medal at the junior world championships, the first time anyone had ever won three medals at that event.

In 1979, LeMond joined the Renault-Gitante team in Europe, and he fell under the coaching tutelage of his teammate, the great French cyclist **Bernard Hinault** (see no 79).

In 1983, LeMond got his first major victory when he won a 169-mile road race in Switzerland with a superb time of 7:1:21. He also won the world professional road racing championship that year.

However, it was in the Tour de France that LeMond made his mark. His first attempt at this grueling race was in 1984, and despite a debilitating bout of bronchitis, he finished in third place—the best showing ever for a non-European cyclist. In the 1985 race, he finished second to Bernard Hinault. Finally, in 1986 LeMond broke through, beating Hinault by more than three minutes and becoming the first American to win the race.

A series of cycling accidents and a near-fatal hunting accident in 1987 put LeMond's career on hold for awhile, but in 1989 he again won the Tour de France—this time by the razor-thin margin of eight seconds. He also won the world professional road racing championship for the second time that year, and was subsequently named Sportsman of the Year by *Sports Illustrated* magazine.

Greg LeMond

In 1990, LeMond won the Tour de France for the third time. However, in the early 1990s, a rare muscular disorder was starting to take its toll on him. He retired from competitive cycling in 1994.

92. Carl Lewis
(1961-) Track and Field

Carl Lewis is one of the greatest all-around track and field athletes in modern history.

Born in Birmingham, Alabama, Lewis went to college at the University of Houston. He won the NCAA long jump championship in 1980, and qualified for the U.S. Olympic team that year. However, when America boycotted the Games as a protest against the Soviet Union's invasion of Afghanistan, Lewis's Olympic dreams, like those of other U.S. athletes, were put on hold.

Lewis did not let up with his relentless training though, and in 1981 he won the NCAA and national outdoor 100-meter and long jump titles. He also won the Sullivan Award that year as the outstanding U.S. amateur athlete.

Lewis continued his outstanding performances in 1982, and in 1983, at the track-and-field world championships in Finland, he won the 100-meter dash and the long jump, and was a member of the winning 4 x 100-meter relay team.

Then came the 1984 Olympics. Lewis put on a spectacular exhibition that year, winning gold medals in the 100- and 200-meter dashes, the long jump, and the 4 x 100-meter relay, duplicating the accomplishment of the immortal **Jesse Owens** (see no. 28) in 1936. With his victory in the 100-meters, Lewis earned the traditional title, the "world's fastest human."

Carl Lewis

Four years later at the 1988 Olympics, Lewis won a gold medal in the long jump and another as a member of victorious 4 x 100 relay team. In the 100-meter dash, he ran a world record time of 9.93 seconds, but finished second to Canadian sprinter **Ben Johnson**. However, Johnson was subsequently found to have used banned substances, was disqualified, and Lewis was declared the winner. Lewis also picked up a silver medal in the 200-meter dash.

At the 1991 track and field world championships in Japan, Lewis proved that he was still the world's fastest man with a record time of 9.86 seconds in the 100-meter dash.

In 1992, Lewis continued his remarkable string of Olympic successes, although he did begin to slow down. He failed to qualify for either the 100 or 200-meter dashes; however, he won a gold medal in the long jump and another as a member of the 4 x 100-meter relay team.

After Lewis hurt his back in a car accident in 1993, his continuation in athletic competition was in doubt. But he surprised his doubters by winning his fourth straight gold medal in the long jump at the 1996 Olympics. This gave him the staggering total of nine gold medals—only the fourth man to accomplish that feat.

Lewis retired from track and field competition in 1997.

Jackie Joyner-Kersee
(1962-) Track and Field

Jackie Joyner-Kersee

Other athletes may have more flash than **Jackie Joyner-Kersee**, but few can match the accomplishments of one of the greatest female track stars of all time.

Jacqueline Joyner was born in East St. Louis, Illinois in 1962. When she was 12, she could broad jump more than 17 feet. At the age of 14, she won the first of four consecutive United States junior national titles in the pentathlon. After she graduated high school, she attended UCLA on a basketball scholarship. There she met coach **Bob Kersee**, who she would marry in 1986.

In 1983, she and her brother Al, who was a triple jumper, represented the United States at the track-and-field world championships in Helsinki, Finland. The following year at the Olympics, she won the silver medal in the heptathlon—a grueling two-day event consisting of the 100-meter hurdles, high jump, shot put, and 200-meter on day one, and the long jump, javelin, and 800-meter race the follow-

ing day; she missed winning the gold medal by .06 seconds.

In 1985, she set an American record in the long jump—23 feet, 9 inches. She set high point totals in several college meets in 1986, scoring 6,910 points at one and 6,841 at another. However, the 7,000-point barrier, never reached by a single athlete, eluded her.

Later that year, though, at the Goodwill Games in Moscow, Joyner-Kersee became the first American woman to hold the world heptathlon record by tallying 7,148 points, shattering the world record by 200 points. She also set an American record of 12.85 seconds in the 100-meter hurdles, and a heptathlon mark of 23 feet in the long jump.

Less than a month later, at the U.S. Olympic Festival in Houston, she broke her own record with 7,161 points, as well as breaking her American long jump record. For her efforts, Joyner-Kersee was named the winner of the Sullivan Award as the country's top amateur athlete.

The victories for this amazing athlete kept coming. At the 1987 Pan-American Games, she equaled the world record in the long jump. Then, in the track and field world championships, she won gold medals in the heptathlon with 7,128 points and the long jump, with a distance of 24 feet, 1 3/4 inches.

Now being hailed as "America's greatest athlete since **Jim Thorpe**," Joyner-Kersee won two gold medals at the 1988 Olympics—in the heptathlon and the long jump. She repeated her gold medal triumph in the heptathlon at the 1992 Olympics, and also took home a bronze in the long jump. She became the first woman to win multi-event titles at two Olympics, and the first athlete of either sex to win multievent medals at three Olympics.

Playing at a position that has seen many, many great athletes over the years, **Jerry Rice** still stands out above all others. He is almost certainly the greatest wide receiver in pro football history.

A native of Starkville, Mississippi, Rice went to school at Mississippi Valley State University, where he became a star. Among the many records he set at the school was a total of 4,693 total yards gained as a receiver. With credentials like that, Rice was destined to go fast in the 1985 National Football League draft, and he did. He was taken in the first round by the San Francisco 49ers—the 16th player drafted.

As a rookie, Rice had some problems holding onto the football, but by his second season, he began to fulfill the 49ers' high expectations of him. In 1986, he led the league with 86 receptions, piling up 1,520 yards, and scoring 15 touchdowns. The following year, he set a single season record for the most touchdowns by a wide receiver with 22. Remarkably, he set that record in a season that was shortened to just 12 games due to a player's strike.

Rice joined a team that had already won two Super Bowl championships in the 1980s, and his presence only added to its offensive weapons, which included quarterback

Jerry Rice

Joe Montana (see no. 82) and running back **Roger Craig**. "Montana-to-Rice" became a familiar cry in the NFL, and the duo led the team to back-to-back Super Bowl victories in 1989 and 1990; Rice was named Super Bowl MVP in the 1989 game. In the early 1990s, when Montana was replaced by Steve Young, Rice became Young's favorite receiver, and the two led the team to another championship in 1995.

Rice became famous for his rigorous training regimen, which included running up the steps of football stadiums. That training kept him in terrific shape; before a knee injury forced him to miss time in 1997, he had appeared in 189 consecutive games.

Rice played for the 49ers through the 1999 season, after which, in both an effort to save money and a belief he was past his prime, they let him go. However, Rice merely moved across the bay to the Oakland Raiders, and continued baffling defensive backs.

By the time the 2002 season began, Rice held career records for most receptions, most receiving yards, most total touchdowns, and most consecutive games with a touchdown. Every time he put on his helmet and pads, he added more yardage to his many records, more detail to his legend, and more evidence to his being the greatest receiver of all time.

Michael Jordan
(1963-) Basketball

By near unanimous consensus, **Michael Jordan** is the greatest all-around pro basketball player in history.

Jordan was born in Brooklyn, New York, and his family moved to Wilmington, North Carolina, when he was very young. As a senior, he led his high school basketball team to 19 wins, and was recruited by legendary coach **Dean Smith** at the University of North Carolina. As a freshman, Jordan hit the winning basket with seconds left in the 1982 NCAA title game to give North Carolina the national championship. Jordan stayed at UNC two more years, and was named college player of the year as a junior.

In 1984, the Chicago Bulls of the National Basketball Association selected Jordan as the third overall pick in the draft, and he immediately revitalized the franchise. In his first year, he led the team in points per game (28.2), rebounds (6.5), assists (5.9), and steals

The cover of a 1996 biography of Michael Jordan

(2.4). He was named the Rookie of the Year and was an All-Star, but the Bulls were eliminated in the playoffs.

That was to be the pattern of Jordan's first few years with the Bulls—great individual play, such as when he scored 63 points in a game or scored over 3,000 points in a season—but team failure in the playoffs.

All that changed, however, when **Phil Jackson** became the Bulls' head coach. With Jackson at the helm, the Bulls won three straight NBA championships, in 1991, 1992 and 1993.

In 1994, Jordan decided he wanted a career change, so he abandoned basketball to play baseball, signing with the Chicago White Sox minor league team. However, after one year Jordan returned to basketball, and the Bulls reeled off three more consecutive NBA championships.

Jordan was a unique player, a man who seemed to defy gravity as he soared through the air to make impossible shots or snatch rebounds. His popularity and commercial appeal were unlimited, and he is credited with pumping up interest in pro basketball to an all-time peak.

In 1999, Jordan retired again. When he left he had scored 29,277 points and amassed 5,836 rebounds. He held the NBA record for the highest career scoring average (31.5 points) and the most seasons leading the league in scoring (10). He was a five-time league MVP, a six-time MVP of the championship finals, and a perennial NBA All-Star.

After two inactive years, the lure of the game proved too much to resist, and Jordan came back in 2001 with the Washington Wizards. Although age and injuries had robbed him of some of his amazing ability, he still showed flashes of the old Michael Jordan on the court.

Matti Nykänen
(1963-) Ski Jumping

The most dominant ski jumper of the 1980s, **Matti Nykänen** was born on September 17, 1963 in Jyväskylä, Finland. His native country's long winter and soaring mountainsides would be ideal for a boy growing up with ambitions of being a ski jumper.

Nykänen received his first pair of skis at the age of nine, and two years later he began competing. By the time he was in the ninth grade, he was so in love with the sport that he quit school to devote more time to training at Lahti Hill in Finland. His hard work and dedication paid off. In 1981, he was the world junior champion. The following year he became the all-time youngest world champion in the 90-meter ski jump.

For Nykänen, all roads led to the 1984 Olympics in Sarajevo, in the former country of Yugoslavia. Expectations for him there were high, and he lived up to them. He put together two near-perfect jumps to win the gold medal in the 90-meter ski jump. His 231.2 total points was 17.5 points ahead of the silver medalist, **Jens Weissflog** of East Germany; it was the largest winning margin in the event in Olympic history. That year Nykänen also won the silver medal in the 70-meter event, as Weissflog won the gold.

Four years later, Nykänen put on an even more impressive

Olympic performance, winning three gold medals at the Games in Calgary, Canada. He took first place in the 90-meter jump with 224 points, and first in the 70-meter jump with 229.1 points. He then won a third gold medal as Finland won the team jumping event. In doing so, Nykänen became the first ski jumper to win the gold in all three events at one Olympics. He was also the first Olympic champion to repeat in a ski jumping event since 1936.

Besides achieving Olympic glory during his career, Nykänen also has four first-place finishes in the World Cup competition to his credit—in 1983, 1985, 1986, and 1988.

Matti Nykänen

Speed skater **Bonnie Blair** has won more Olympic gold medals than any other American female athlete.

Although she was born in Cornwall, New York, she grew up in Champaign, Illinois, the unofficial speed skating capital in the United States. All six Blair children skated competitively, and four of Blair's siblings grew up to be national champions.

At the age of six, Blair won races against nine and ten-year old girls. At seven, she competed in the short-track speed skating state championships. In 1979, Blair met Olympic gold medalist and speed skating coach **Cathy Faminow**, who encouraged her to work on her speed skating year-round. In 1980, Blair decided to concentrate on Olympic-style racing—in which two skaters are on the track, racing against time rather than one another—instead of short track.

Even though she was nationally ranked, in 1982, Blair was advised to train in Europe. She was short of funds, so the local police department held a series of raffles and bake sales so she could obtain the money. Blair received much needed experience in Olympic-style skating during her time in Europe.

Blair won the U.S. indoor title in 1983, 1984, and 1986, and was the North American indoor champion in 1985. After setting a world record time in the 500-meter event at the 1987 word championships, Blair was ready for the Winter Olympic Games the following year.

In the 1988 Games in Calgary, Canada, Blair won the gold medal in the 500-meter race with a blazing time of 39.1 seconds. When she also won the bronze medal in the 1,000-meter, she became the only American athlete to win more than one medal at that year's Olympics.

However, Blair's Olympic triumphs were just beginning. At the 1992 Games, she again

Bonnie Blair

won the 500-meter race, and also picked up a gold in the 1,000-meter race, which she won by only two hundredths of a second. She also became the first woman from any nation to win consecutive gold medals in the 500-meter race.

Then in 1994, at the Games in Lilehammer, Norway, she did it again, winning the gold medal in both the 500-meter and 1,000-meter races. This gave her five golds, more than any other American female Olympic athlete. With her total of six overall medals, she surpassed **Eric Heiden's** Winter Olympics medal record of five, giving her the most medals of any U.S. Winter Olympian.

Blair accrued other honors as well during her career. In 1992, she received the Sullivan Award, which is given to the outstanding American amateur athlete of the year.

In 1995, Blair retired from competitive skating.

98. Barry Bonds
(1964-) Baseball

A rare combination of great power and outstanding speed, **Barry Bonds** rewrote baseball's record book several times over at an age when most players are just about to retire from the game.

Bonds was born in Riverside, California, with baseball blood flowing in his veins. His father was **Bobby Bonds**, who combined speed and power when he played for several teams in the 1970s and 1980s. His godfather is **Willie Mays**, perhaps the greatest outfielder in baseball history.

Bonds was drafted by the Pittsburgh Pirates and joined them in May 1986. His break-out season was in 1990, when he hit .301, with 33 homers and 114 RBI, and was named the National League's Most Valuable Player.

Led by Bonds, the Pirates became dominant in the N.L.'s Eastern Division in the early 1990s, winning the title three years in a row. However, the team couldn't get past the first round of the divisional playoffs, and Bonds had poor post-seasons. Finally, after another MVP season in 1992, Bonds left the Pirates and signed a large free agent contract with the San Francisco Giants.

In his first season with the Giants, Bonds was outstanding, hitting .336 with 46 homers and 123 RBI. He was again voted the league MVP. Bonds continued to put up great numbers with the Giants during the 1990s, but although the team made three playoff appearances, they couldn't get to the World Series.

Then in 2001, Bonds had an historic season, breaking **Mark McGwire's** single-season record of 70 home runs with 73; he also hit .328, drove in 137 runs, and set a new single-season slugging percentage of .863, breaking **Babe Ruth's** 82-year old mark. He also walked 177 times, breaking another long-standing Ruth record, and won an unprecedented fourth MVP award.

The following year Bonds continued to show that he was getting better with age, by leading the league in batting with a .370 mark, smashing 46 homers, and winning his fifth MVP. He also finally made it to his first World Series, and while the Giants lost in seven games to the California Angels, Bonds exorcised the ghostly failures of post-seasons past with a Series average of .471, with 4 home runs and 6 RBI.

As the 2003 season began, Bonds was still going strong; in June that year, he became the first player in history to hit 500 home runs and steal 500 bases. By mid-season, his career home run total stood at more than 650, and some people were beginning to say that he had a chance of breaking **Hank Aaron's** mark of 755 homers one day. Either way, Bonds's reservation in baseball's Hall of Fame has already been secured.

Barry Bonds

99. Lance Armstrong
(1971-) Cycling

The word "courageous" can be defined in several different ways, but surely that word can be applied to **Lance Armstrong**, the American cyclist who has won the Tour de France a record-tying five times.

He was born in Plano, Texas, and mainly raised by his mother. Armstrong was attracted to athletics at an early age, and by the age of 13 he was competing in triathlons. Three years later, he was good enough to turn professional.

Lance Armstrong

However, cycling was proving more alluring than swimming or running—the other athletic events comprising the triathlon—and Armstrong was soon devoting all his energies to it. The national cycling club took notice of this dedicated youngster, and invited him to work with them while he was a senior in high school.

Armstrong qualified for the 1989 junior world championship in Moscow in the summer following his high school graduation. Two years later, he was the United States

National Amateur Champion. He also won two other cycling races that year —the First Union Grand Prix and the Thrifty Drug Classic.

In August 1993, Armstrong became the youngest person in history to win the world race championships in Oslo, Norway. The following year, he was the runner-up in the Tour Du Pont. Then in 1995, he won the race by posting the largest margin of victory in its history.

Armstrong soon was facing a challenge beyond any mere cycling race. In October 1996, after signing a lucrative sponsorship contract, he learned that he had testicular cancer, which had spread to his brain and lungs. He was given a forty percent chance of recovery. He lost his sponsorship contract.

It was then that this determined man showed what he was made of. Thanks to a rigorous chemotherapy program and surgery, he was pronounced healthy in February 1997. He then began training, determined to scale the heights of the cycling world once again. With the sponsorship muscle of the U.S. Postal Service behind him, Armstrong won several races in 1998 as he slowly climbed back into the competitive cycling mainstream.

Then in 1999, Armstrong wrote the sweetest possible conclusion to his comeback story by winning the world's premier bicycle race, the Tour de France. However, that was just the first of his five successive victories in the event—tying the career record for wins held by four other cyclists, and equaling the consecutive-win record of **Miguel Indurain**.

After he was diagnosed with cancer, Armstrong established the Lance Armstrong Foundation which has helped to advance cancer research, diagnosis, treatment, and aftertreatment services. Having beaten his cancer, Armstrong wanted to help others succeed in this toughest fight of all.

100. Tiger Woods
(1975-) Golf

In a sport filled with legendary names and careers— Jones, Nicklaus, Palmer—the name of **Tiger Woods** might one day be the most legendary of all.

Eldrick Woods was born in 1975 in Orange County, California. He was nick-named Tiger after a Vietnamese soldier who was a friend of his father's. When he was ten months old, he would watch his father hit golf balls into a net for hours. A true child prodigy, when he was three years old, he shot a 48 for nine holes. Two years later, he was featured in *Golf Digest* magazine.

When Woods was seven, his father had him listening to subliminal tapes to improve his mental game. His father would also try his hardest to distract Woods while he was swing-ing, in order to teach him mental toughness.

Woods attended Stanford University, and played on the golf team. Along the way he won numerous amateur tournaments. He won the U.S. Junior Amateur championship three years in a row (1991-193), when no one before had ever won more than one. He was named the top amateur player by *Golf Digest*, *Golfweek*, and *Golf World* in 1992 and 1993. In 1996, he won the National Collegiate Athletic Association (NCAA) championship, and was the collegiate player of the year.

In 1996, Woods turned pro and immedi-ately had success, notching two victories and three top ten finishes in his first eight starts. His first Professional Golfers Association (PGA) win came at the Las Vegas Invitational. That year he was the PGA Tour Rookie of the Year. He was also named *Sports Illustrated's* Sportsman of the Year.

Since then, Woods has become the most dominant player in professional golf. In 1997, he was the PGA Tour Player of the Year, winning four tournaments and finishing in the top ten in nine others. He also set a 72-hole record at the Masters Tournament with a 270. In 1999, Woods earned over $6 million, nearly three million more than his nearest competitor.

The following year Woods had one of the greatest seasons in golf history. He won the U.S. and British Opens, as well as the PGA championship, giving him all four grand slam titles at the unbelievable age of 25. He won nine PGA tournaments, and earned a record of more than $8 million.

By the year 2002, Woods had won eight grand slam tournaments, and given his age, had a legitimate chance to become the all-time grand slam tournament record holder. Before he retires, many people predict he will hold every major golf record that can be set.

Tiger Woods

TRIVIA QUIZ & PROJECTS

Test your knowledge and challenge your friends with the following questions. The answers are contained in the biographies noted.

1. Which sport is a famous Roman emperor credited with establishing as a pastime? (see no. 4)
2. Who overcame a childhood disease that left him confined to a wheelchair and later became an Olympic champion? (see no. 9)
3. Why did a "long count" in a boxing match cost a fighter his chance to regain the heavyweight championship of the world? (see no. 18)
4. How did a legendary college running back help professional football gain widespread acceptance with the public? (see no. 23)
5. Which Olympic track and field star later became one of the world's greatest women golfers? (see no. 25)
6. When did the athletic performance of a black American track and field star shatter the racial theories of a world leader? (see no. 28)
7. Who do many baseball experts consider to be the greatest hitter ever to play the game? (see no. 33)
8. How did one long-time Montreal Canadien goalie significantly influence the sport of hockey? (see no. 42)
9. Where did one of pro basketball's greatest centers first get national recognition as an outstanding collegiate player? (see no. 51)
10. Why was one of baseball's most dominant pitchers forced to retire at the height of his career? (see no. 53)
11. Who is the only tennis player to have twice won all four Grand Slam tournaments in one year? (see no. 57)
12. Which boxer is the only fighter ever to hold the world heavyweight championship three times? (see no. 62)
13. How did a skier who never had a skiing lesson in her life win six World Cup titles during the 1970s? (see no. 75)
14. When did a championship tennis star become the oldest person ever to win a grand slam event? (see no. 83)
15. Which speed skater holds more Olympic medals than any other American female athlete? (see no. 97)
16. Who overcame a life-threatening illness to become a world champion cyclist? (see no. 99)

Suggested Projects

1. Choose one of the athletes from this book and write a one-page fictional diary entry for one day in that person's life. Pick a day that had some significance for the individual; for example, the day he or she had a great performance in an athletic event or achieved some other noteworthy success. Or choose a day on which the person met with a personal setback, or was frustrated in some way by a lack of success. Describe the person's thoughts and feelings with as much detail as you can.

2. Arrange a "meeting" of two of the people in this book who could never have met in real life. You can choose two athletes from the same sport who never competed against each other, or two from different fields of athletic competition, but they must be from different eras. (For example, Babe Ruth and Willie Mays, or Babe Didrikson-Zaharias and Martina Navratilova.) Imagine what their meeting would be like. Write 1-2 pages describing the scenario of their meeting, and create dialogue between the two people. What kinds of questions do you think they would ask each other? Would they approve of the things that each had done in their lifetimes? Be as imaginative as you can.

Index

Index

Index

Index